Sir John Fortescue's
The Cruelest Necessity

Sir John Fortescue's
The Cruelest Necessity

The British Army, the English Civil War and the
Conflicts of the 17th Century

J. W. Fortescue

LEONAUR

Sir John Fortescue's The Cruelest Necessity
The British Army, The English Civil War and the Conflicts of the 17th Century
by J. W. Fortescue

FIRST EDITION

First published under the title
A History of the British Army Vol 1 & 2 (Extracts)

Leonaur is an imprint of Oakpast Ltd

ISBN: 978-1-78282-361-2 (hardcover)
ISBN: 978-1-78282-362-9 (softcover)

http://www.leonaur.com

Publisher's Notes

Contents

CHAPTER 1

Cadiz

Of the reign of James the First, (1603-1625), there is little to be recorded concerning the British Army except that at its very outset the Statute of Philip and Mary for the regulation of the Militia was repealed, and the military organisation of the country based once more on the Statute of Winchester. James was not fond of soldiers, and military progress was not to be expected of such a man. Enough has already been seen of his methods through his dealings with the Low Countries, and there is no occasion to dwell on the first British king of the ill-fated House of Stuart.

Charles the First was more ambitious, and sufficiently proud of the English soldier to preserve the ancient English drum-march. Soon after the final breach with Spain he imbibed from Buckingham the idea of a raid on the Spanish coast after the Elizabethan model, which eventually took shape in the expedition to Cadiz. Of all the countless mismanaged enterprises in our history this seems on the whole to have been the very worst. There was abundance of trained soldiers in England who had learned their duty in the Low Countries; and Edward Cecil, whom some few years back, in command of the cavalry at Nieuport, begged that liberal offers might be made to induce them to serve. Officers again could be procured from the Low Countries, and therefore there should have been no difficulty in organising an excellent body of men. In the matter of arms, however, though English cannon was highly esteemed, Charles was forced to purchase what he needed from Holland, which was a sad reflection on our national enterprise.

Accordingly over a hundred officers were recalled from Holland; and two thousand recruits were collected, to be sent in exchange for the same number of veterans from the Dutch service. Eight thousand men were then pressed for service in various parts of England, and the whole of them poured, without the least preparation to receive them, into Plymouth, where they gained for themselves the name of the plagues of England. Sir John Ogle, a veteran who had served for years with Francis Vere, eyed these recruits narrowly for a time, old, lame, sick and destitute men for the most part, and reflected how without stores, clothes, or money he could possibly convert them into soldiers. Then taking his resolution he threw up his command and took refuge in the Church. Very soon another difficulty arose. The States-General firmly refused to accept two thousand raw men in exchange for veterans, and shipped the unhappy recruits back to England. They too were turned into Plymouth and made confusion worse confounded. Then the arms arrived from Holland, and there was no money to pay men to unload them.

The port became a chaos. Buckingham had already shuffled out of the chief command and saddled it on Cecil, and the unfortunate man, good soldier though he was, was driven to his wit's end to cope with his task. His tried officers from Holland were displaced to make room for Buckingham's favourites, who were absolutely useless; and yet he was expected to clothe, arm, train, discipline, and organise ten thousand raw, naked men, work out every detail of a difficult and complicated expedition, and make every provision for it, all without help, without encouragement, and without money. Cash indeed was so scarce that the king could not afford to pay the expenses of his own journey to Plymouth.

Under such conditions it is hardly surprising that the enterprise was a disastrous failure. A few butts of liquor left by the Spaniards outside Cadiz sufficed to set the whole force fighting with its own officers, and after weary weeks at sea, aggravated by heavy weather and by pestilence, the result of bad stores, Cecil and the remains of his ten regiments returned home in misery and shame. [1]

A similar enterprise under Lord Willoughby in the following year failed in the same way for precisely the same reasons; but Buckingham, still unshaken in his confidence, led a third and a fourth expedition to Rochelle with equal disaster and equal disgrace. The captains had no more control over their men than over a herd of deer. [2] At last, at the outset of a fifth expedition, which promised similar failure, the dagger of Lieutenant Felton, a melancholy man embittered by deprivation of

1. Mr. Dalton has told the story very fully in his *Life of Cecil*.
2. Ward, *Animadversions of Warre.*

his pay, put an end to Buckingham and to all his follies. On the whole he had not treated the soldiers worse than Elizabeth, but a man of Elizabeth's stamp was more than could be borne with.

Nevertheless, amid all these failures there were still plenty of men in England who had the welfare of the military profession at heart. Foremost among them was the veteran Edward Cecil, now Lord Wimbledon, who strove hard to do something for the defence of the principal ports, for the training of the nation at large, and in particular for the encouragement of cavalry. The mounted service had become strangely unpopular with the English at this time, whether because the eternal sieges of the Dutch war afforded it less opportunity of distinction, or because missile tactics had lowered it from its former proud station, it is difficult to say. Certain it is that officers of infantry, and notably Monro, never lost an opportunity of girding at horsemen as fitted only to run away, and as preferring to be mounted only that they might run away the faster.

But Cecil, though in this respect unique, was by no means the only man who made his voice heard. Veteran after veteran took pen in hand and wrote of the discipline of Maurice of Nassau and, as time went on, of the system of Gustavus Adolphus; while on the other hand one ingenious gentleman, still jealous of the old national weapon, invented what he called a "double-arm," which combined the pike and the bow, the bow-staff being attached to the shaft of the pike by a vice which could be traversed on a hinge. Strange to say this belated weapon was not ill-received in military circles and found commendation even among Scotsmen. [3]

On one important point, however, there was a general consensus of opinion, namely that the condition of the English militia was disgraceful, its system hopelessly inefficient and the corruption of its administration a scandal. The trained bands were hardly called out once in five years for exercise; few men knew how even to load their muskets, and the majority were afraid to fire a shot except in salute of the colours, not daring to fire a bullet from want of practice. [4] The Londoners, as usual, alone made a favourable exception to the general rule.

---

3. See *Pallas Armata*, by Sir T. Kellie, 1627. This writer deserves mention as the first who introduced the system of drilling by numbers. He talks as glibly of odd and even numbers as a modern drill sergeant.
4. Barriffe and Ward.

The real root of the evil was presently to be laid bare. The disputes between Charles the First and his subjects were assuming daily an acuter form, until at last they came to a head in the Scotch rebellion of 1639. It was imperative to raise an English force forthwith and move it up to the Border. Charles, as usual in the last stage of impecuniosity, thought to save money by an exercise of old feudal rights, and summoned every peer with his retinue to attend him in person as his principal force of cavalry. It was a piece of tactless folly whereof none but a Stuart would have been guilty: the peers came in some numbers as they were bid, but they did not conceal their resentment against such proceedings.

The foot were levied as usual by writ to the lord-lieutenant with the help of the press-gang, they behaved abominably on their march to the rendezvous, and on arrival were found to be utterly inefficient. Their arms were of all sorts, sizes, and calibres, and the men were so careless in the handling of them that hardly a tent in the camp, not even the king's, escaped perforation by stray bullets. In other respects the organisation was equally deficient; no provision had been made for the supply of victuals and forage; and altogether it was fortunate that the force escaped, through the pacification of Berwick, an engagement with the veterans from the Swedish service under old Alexander Leslie that composed a large portion of the Scottish Army.

The following year saw the war renewed. This time the farce of calling out a feudal body of horse was not repeated, but unexpected difficulties were encountered in raising the levies of foot. In 1639 the infantry had been drawn chiefly from the northern counties, where the tradition of eternal feuds with the Scots made men not altogether averse to a march to the Border. But in 1640 the trained bands of the southern counties were called upon, and they had no such feeling. It is possible that unusual rigour was employed in the process of impressment, for the authorities had been warned, after experience of the previous year, to allow no captains to play the Falstaff with their recruits. Be that as it may, the recalcitrance of the new levies was startling.

From county after county came complaints of riot and disorder. The Wiltshire men seized the opportunity to live by robbery and plunder; the Dorsetshire men murdered an officer who had corrected a drummer for flagrant insubordination; in Suffolk the recruits threatened to murder the deputy-lieutenant; in London, Kent, Surrey, and half a dozen more counties the resistance to service was equally determined; and when finally in July four thousand men reached the rendezvous at Selby, old Sir Jacob Astley could only designate them as the arch-knaves of the country. Money being of course very scarce, the men were ill-clothed and ill-found, and their numbers were soon thinned by systematic desertion.

A new difficulty cropped up in the matter of discipline. Lord Conway, who commanded the horse, had executed a man for mutiny; he now found that his action was illegal and that he required the royal pardon. If, he wrote, the lawyers are right and martial law is impossible in England, it would be best to break up the army forthwith: to hand men over to the civil power is to deliver them to the lawyers, and experience of the ship-money has shown what support could be expected from them.

There, in fact, lay the kernel of the whole matter; indiscipline was not only rife in the ranks but widespread throughout the nation. From long carelessness and neglect the organisation of the country for defence by land and sea had become not only obsolete but impossible and absurd. For centuries the old vessel had been patched and tinkered and filed and riveted, occasionally by statute, more often by royal authority only, but chiefly by mere habit and custom. But now that the reaction which had established the new monarchy was over, and men, stirred by a counter-reaction, subjected the military system to the fierce heat of constitutional tests, the whole fabric fell asunder in an instant, and brought the new monarchy down headlong in its fall. The story is so instructive to a nation which has not yet given its standing army a permanent statutory existence, that it is worth while very briefly to trace the progress of the catastrophe.

According to ancient practice, the various shires were called upon to provide their levies for the Scotch war with coat-money and with conduct-money to pay their expenses till they had passed the borders of the county, from which moment they passed into the king's pay. The writs to the lord-lieutenants distinctly stated that these charges would be refunded from the Royal Exchequer, and though the chronic emptiness of the Royal Exchequer might diminish the value of the pledge, the form of the writ was distinctly consonant with custom and precedent. Many of the county gentlemen, however, refused to pay this coat- and conduct-money; they had been encouraged by the attacks made on military charges in the Short Parliament; and the Crown, aware of the general opposition to all its doings, did not venture to prosecute.

11

Another incident raised the general question of military obligations in an acuter form. In August 1640, Charles, sadly hampered by the general objections to military service on any terms, fell back on the old system of issuing Commissions of Array to the lord-lieutenants and sheriffs. In themselves Commissions of Array, especially when addressed to these particular officers, were nothing extraordinary; they had been in use to the reign of Queen Mary, and though more or less superseded by the appointment of lord-lieutenants, were by implication sanctioned by a statute of Henry the Fourth.

Now, however, these Commissions at once raised a storm. The deputy-lieutenants of Devon promptly approached the Council with an awkward dilemma. To which service, they asked, were the gentry to attach themselves, to the trained bands or to the feudal service implied in the Commissions of Array; since both were equally enjoined by proclamation? The Council answered that the service in the trained bands must be personal, and the feudal obligation satisfied by deputy or by pecuniary composition; in other words, if the gentry halted between two services, they could not go wrong in performing both. A second question from the deputy-lieutenants was still more searching: how were the bands levied under the Commissions to be paid? The reply of the Council pointed out that the laws and customs of the realm required every man, in the event of invasion, to serve for the common defence at his own charge. Here Charles was strictly within his rights; and the plea of invasion was sound, since the Scots had actually passed the Tweed.

Parliament, however, seized hold of the Commissions of Array, and after innumerable arguments as to their illegality, took final refuge under the Petition of Right. Stripped of all redundant phrases, the position of the two parties was this: Charles asked how he could raise an army for defence of the kingdom, if the powers enjoyed by his predecessors were stripped from him; and Parliament answered that it had no intention of allowing him any power whatever to raise such an army.

The campaign in the north was speedily ended, (August 28th), by the advance of the Scots and by the rout of the small English detachment that guarded the fords of the Tyne at Newburn. The Scots then occupied Newcastle, and England to all intent lay at their mercy. Nothing could have better suited the opponents of the king. A treaty was patched up at Ripon which amounted virtually to an agreement to subsidise the Scotch Army in the interest of the Parliament. The

Scots consented to stay where they were in consideration of eight hundred and fifty pounds a day, failing the payment of which it was open to them to continue their march southward and impose their own terms. Charles could not possibly raise such a sum without recourse to Parliament, and the assembly with which he had now to do was that which is known to history as the Long Parliament.

Within seven months it had passed an Act to prevent its dissolution without its own consent, and having thus secured itself, it allowed the English Army to be disbanded, while the Scots, having played their part, retired once more across the Tweed.

ENGLAND & WALES
May 1st 1643
Districts held by the King
Do   Do   Parliament

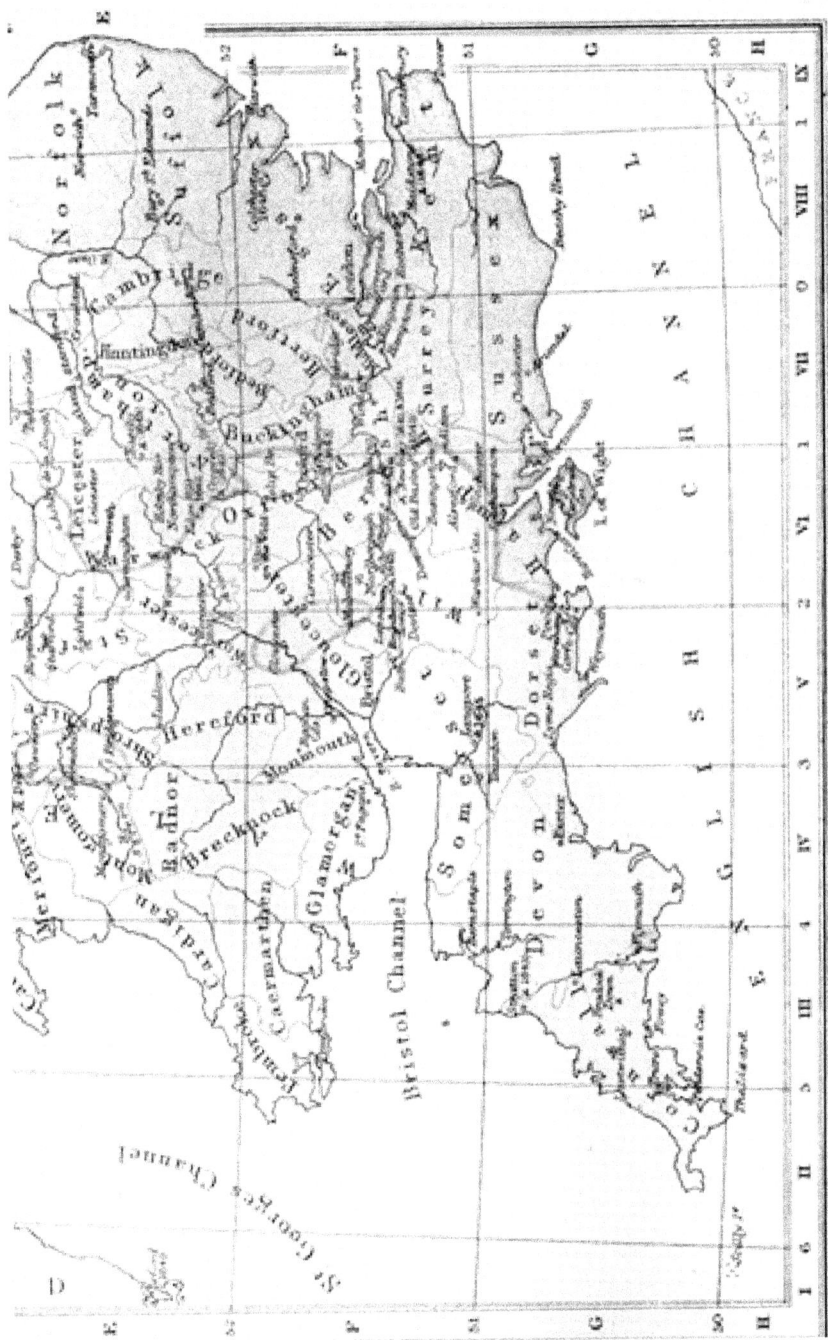

CHAPTER 2

Maston Moor

It would be tedious to follow the widening of the breach between King and Parliament during the year 1641. Both parties saw that war was inevitable, and both struggled hard to keep the militia each in its own hands. The scramble was supremely ridiculous, since it was all for a prize not worth the snatching. Charles has been censured for throwing the whole military organisation out of gear because he wished to employ it for other objects than the safety of the kingdom, but it would be difficult, I think, for an one to explain what military organisation existed. By the showing of the Parliamentary lawyers themselves, there was no statute to regulate it except the Statute of Winchester; in strictness there was no legal requirement for men to equip themselves otherwise than as in the year 1285. It was to the party that first made an army, not to that which preferred the sounder claim to regulate the militia, that victory was to belong. Strafford had perceived this long before, but three years were yet to pass before Parliament should realise it.

The few movements worth noting in the scramble may be very briefly summarised. The king reluctantly consented to transfer the power of impressment to the justices of the peace with approval of Parliament, and abandoned his right to compel men to service outside their counties. But he refused to concede to Parliament the nomination of lord-lieutenants or the custody of strong places, and Parliament therefore simply arrogated to itself these privileges without further question. In July the Commons resolved to levy an army of ten thousand men, in August the king unfurled the Royal Standard at Nottingham; and so the Civil War began.

The lists of the two opposing armies of 1642 are still extant: the king's, of fourteen regiments of foot and eighteen troops of horse, and the Parliament's, of eighteen regiments of foot, seventy-five troops of horse, and five troops of dragoons; but it would be unprofitable to linger over them, for except on paper they were not armies at all. Two names however must be noticed. The first is that of the commander of the Royal Horse, Prince Rupert, a son of the Winter-King. He had now been domiciled in England for seven years, in the course of which he had found time to serve the Dutch, as at the siege of Breda in 1639, and the Swedes in the following year, commanding with the latter a regiment of horse in more than one dashing engagement. He was now three-and-twenty, not an unripe age for a general in those days, as Condé was presently to prove at Rocroi. The second name is that of the captain of the Sixty-Seventh troop of the Parliamentary horse, Oliver Cromwell, a gentleman of Huntingdon, not inconspicuous as a member of Parliament but unknown to military fame. He was already forty-three years of age, and so far was little familiar with the profession of arms.[1]

On the 23rd of October these two men met at Edgehill, the first important action of the war, on which I shall not dwell further than to notice the part that they played therein. Rupert, knowing the deficiency of fire-arms in the royal cavalry, before the battle gave his horsemen orders to keep their ranks and to attack sword in hand, not attempting to use their pistols till they had actually broken into the enemy's squadrons. Here was an improvement on the Swedish system, a step nearer to shock-action, which was crowned by complete success. Oliver Cromwell having seen the havoc wrought by the Royalist cavalry, sought and found after the battle the cause of the inferiority of the Parliament's. He said to John Hampden:

Your troops are most of them old decayed serving-men and tapsters: their troops are gentlemen's sons and persons of quality. Do you think the spirits of such base and mean fellows will ever be able to encounter gentlemen who have courage, honour, and resolution in them? You must get men of a spirit that is likely to go as far as gentlemen will go, or you will be beaten still.

Hampden heard and shook his head; he was a wise and worthy person, but he had probably an idea that no men except such as those which had been swept into the ranks by the king and the king's father

---

1. His name indeed appears as an ensign in the list of a company of foot raised for service in Ireland (printed in June 1642), but this does not count for much.

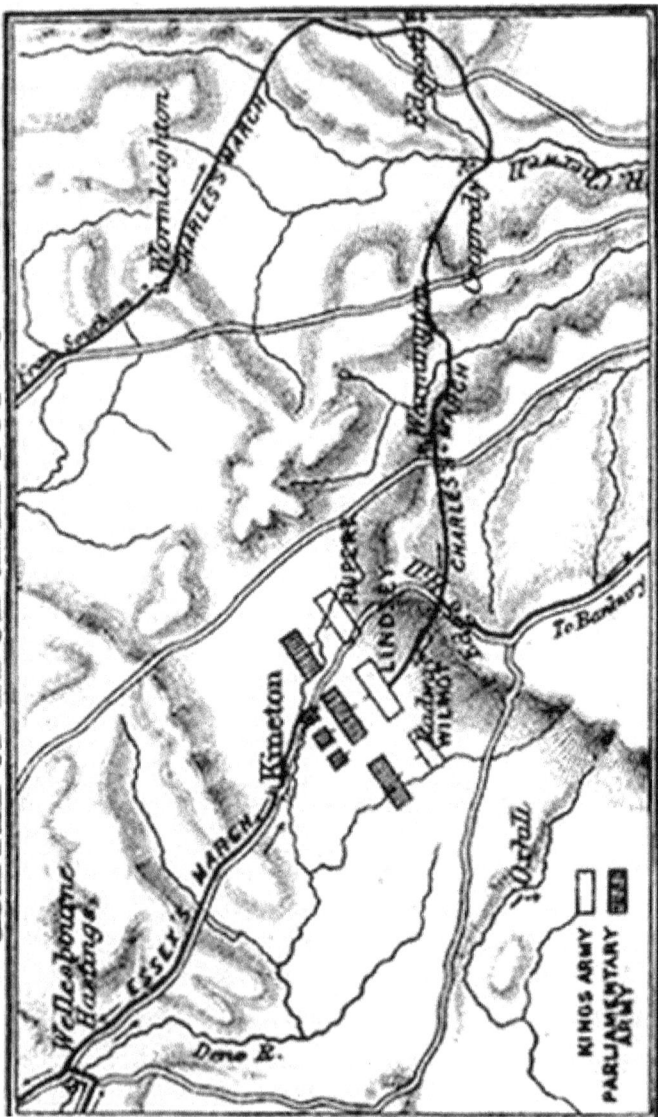

BATTLE OF EDGE HILL OCT. 23rd 1642.

KINGS ARMY
PARLIAMENTARY ARMY

Scale of Miles

could possibly be induced to become soldiers. So he said that it was a good notion but impracticable. Captain Cromwell set to work to show that it was not impracticable, and began to raise men who, in his own words, made some conscience of what they did, and to teach them discipline.

Meanwhile the helplessness of the Parliament in the early stages of the war was almost ludicrous; and though indeed few things are more remarkable than the rapid growth of administrative ability between the years 1642 and 1658, it must be admitted that at first the civil leaders of the people were little better than children. Nearly the whole nation, and with it the majority of legislators, had made up their minds that the first battle would decide the contest, and they were woefully disappointed when it did not do so. Failing at first to realise the elementary principle that money is the sinew of war the Houses trusted at first to irregular contributions for its support, nor was it until pressed to extremity that they determined to employ general taxation. Money was the first and eternal difficulty, which however pressed even harder on the king than on the Parliament.

The next obstacle was the utter collapse of the existing military organisation. The county levies were ready enough to fight in defence of their own homes, but they were unwilling to move far from them; and when the enemy had left their own particular quarter they thanked God that they were rid of him and returned to their usual avocations. This again was a difficulty that beset both sides and was never overcome by the king. The Parliament tried to meet it by the establishment of associations of counties, which were virtually military districts, and did something, though not much, to widen the narrow sympathies of the militiamen. But these associations, though a step in the right direction, depended too much on the individual energy of the men at their head to attain uniform success; and one only, the Eastern, wherein Cromwell was the moving spirit, did for a time really efficient work.

A third and most formidable danger was the superiority of the Royalist cavalry. The long neglect of the mounted service left the supremacy to the ablest amateurs, and the majority of these, though there were hundreds of gentlemen on the Parliamentary side, were undoubtedly for the king. Nor was it only the courage, honour, and resolution of which Cromwell had spoken that favoured them; they had from the nature of the case better horses, a higher standard of horsemanship and equipment, a quicker natural intelligence and a higher natural training.

BATTLE OF
MARSTON MOOR
July 2nd 1644

ENGLISH MILES

Royalist.
Parliamentary.

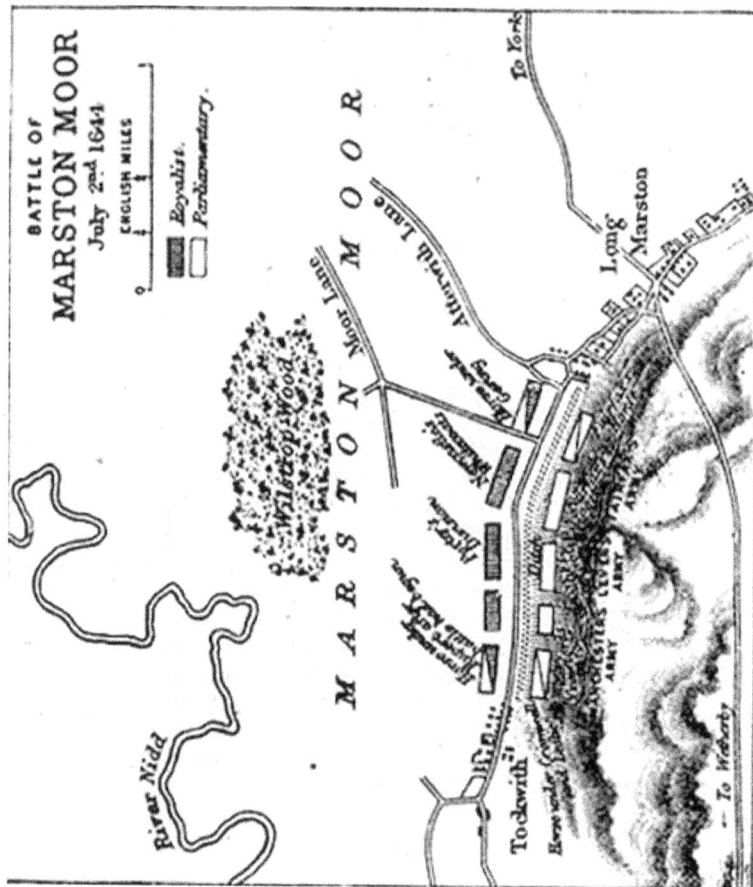

MARSTON MOOR

River Nidd

Wilstrop Wood

Marston Moor Lane

Atterwith Lane

To York

Long Marston

Tockwith

LESLIE'S (?) ARMY

To Wetherby

The thousand lessons which the county gentlemen learned when riding with hawk and hound were of infinite advantage in the casual and irregular warfare of the first two or three years; and whatever may be said of Rupert's ability on the battlefield, there can be no question that the work of his innumerable patrols was admirably done. The dashing character of Rupert was also an advantage in a sense to the king's cause, for it attracted to him a group of fellow hot-heads similar to those that had followed Thomas Felton under the Black Prince. One fatal defect however marred what should have been a most efficient cavalry, the blot that had been hit by Cromwell, indiscipline.

The campaign of 1643 found Parliament little wiser than before as to the true method of conducting a war. Though it had named Lord Essex as general it gave him no control over the operations of any army but his own, and there was consequently no unity either of design or of purpose. Charles, on the contrary, had a definite plan, which had been mapped out for him by some unknown hand and was within an ace of successful execution. He himself with one army fixed his headquarters at Oxford; a second army under Newcastle was to advance from the north, a third under Prince Maurice and Sir Ralph Hopton from the extreme west, both converging on Charles as a centre; and the united forces were then to advance on London. Hopton, an experienced soldier and as noble a man as fought in the war, executed his part brilliantly, advancing victoriously into Somerset from Cornwall, and finally defeating the force specially sent to meet him by the Parliament at Roundway Down.

This action is memorable for the appearance, and it must be added the defeat, of what was probably the last fully mailed troop of horse ever seen in England, Sir Arthur Hazelrigg's "Lobsters," so called from the hardness of their shells. Hopton's advance was only stayed by the unwillingness of his Western levies to move any further from their homes. In the north again the Parliament had suffered disaster; the Fairfaxes, who were the mainstay of the cause, sustained a crushing defeat, and but one man stood in the way to bar Newcastle's march upon London.

That man however was Oliver Cromwell. Already he had begun to put in practice the scheme which Hampden had pronounced impracticable. He had chosen his recruits from the Puritan yeomen and farmers of the Eastern Counties, men who had thrown themselves heart and soul into the religious struggles of the time, who made some conscience of what they did, "who knew what they were fighting for and loved what they knew," and who thought it honourable to submit to rigid discipline for so noble a cause. Cromwell was now a colonel, and he had already shown the mettle of his force, while it was still incomplete, by defeating a body of twice its numbers in a skirmish at Grantham. This too he had done not by any novelty in tactics, for he admits that he attacked only at a pretty round trot, but by superiority of handling and of discipline. With the same troops strengthened and improved he now advanced and met a strong force of Newcastle's advanced horse at Gainsborough; and by skilful manoeuvring and full appreciation of the principle, as yet unwritten, that in the combat of cavalry victory rests with him that throws in the last reserves, he routed it completely.

Following up his success he came, unexpectedly as he admits, upon the main body of Newcastle's army, both horse and foot. Horses and men were weary after a hard day's work and a long pursuit, but they showed a bold front; and Cromwell, drawing them off by alternate bodies, once again a movement which was not to be found in the text-books, [2] safely effected his retreat. In truth the man was a born soldier, and probably a great deal fonder of the profession of arms, late though he had entered upon it, than he would have cared to admit. "I have a lovely company," he wrote shortly after this action, with the genuine pride of a good regimental officer; and in spite of the rigour of his discipline his troops increased until they were sufficient to fill two complete regiments.

The danger from the north was averted for the moment, but the situation was so critical that the Parliament authorised the impressment of men and raised Essex's army to a respectable total. But meanwhile negotiations had been opened with the Scots for the advance of their army against the king's forces in the north, and by September the conditions, military, financial, and religious, were agreed upon. This treaty brought home to the Parliament the necessity for immediately opening up its communications with the north and making a way whereby the Scots might penetrate further southward. The difficult task was achieved by the united efforts of two men who here fought their first action together, Thomas Fairfax and Oliver Cromwell. The day of Winceby must for this reason remain memorable in the history of the army, not the less so because it brought Cromwell nearer to his death than any action before or after it.

---

2. I have however found an early instance of it in the French religious wars, but have unfortunately mislaid the reference.

By the close of the year Parliament began to realise that if the war were to be carried to a successful issue, some more effective force than mere trained bands must be called into existence. It accordingly voted that Essex's army should be fixed at a permanent establishment of ten thousand foot and four thousand horse with a regular rate of monthly pay. This was progress in the right direction, but in the disorder of the financial administration it was extremely doubtful whether the scheme would not be wrecked by its cost. Meanwhile the Scots had crossed the Tweed and fairly entered as partners with the Parliament in the rebellion.

This new factor led to the formation of a Committee of Both Kingdoms for the subsequent conduct of the war, an important step towards unity of design and administration but clogged by one fatal defect, namely, that the military members—Essex, Manchester, Waller, and Cromwell—were all absent in the field, and that the direction of operations therefore fell entirely into the hands of civilians. A Committee was better than a whole House, and that was all that could be said, for the new directorate soon came into collision with its officers in the field. On the invasion of the Scots, Charles of necessity altered his plan of campaign and detached Rupert to the north, who marked the line of his advance in deeper than ordinary lines of desolation and bloodshed. The Parliamentary generals in the north, Fairfax and Manchester, were at the time engaged upon the siege of York. The Committee, scared by the terror of Rupert's march, ordered them to raise the siege and move southward to meet him. They flatly refused; and their persistence in their own design led to the greatest military success hitherto achieved by the Parliament, the victory of Marston Moor.

Of no battle are contemporary accounts more difficult of reconciliation than those of Marston Moor, but the main features of the action are distinguishable and may be briefly set down. Both armies consisted of about twenty-three thousand men, and were drawn up in two lines, the infantry in the centre and the cavalry in the flanks. On the Royalist side Rupert, as was usual for the commander-in-chief, led the right wing, [3] five thousand horse in one hundred troops; his centre, fourteen thousand foot, was under Eythin, a veteran officer imported from Germany; his left, four thousand cavalry, was led by Goring.

---

3. He is said to have posted himself opposite Cromwell, but he only took his usual place at the right of the line; he occupied the same position at Naseby and took no pains to meet Cromwell there.

ENGLAND & WALES

January 1st 1644.

Districts held by the King ——
Do Do Parliament ——

NORTH SEA

SCOTLAND

IRISH SEA

I. of Man

IRELAND

Glasgow

Edinburgh

Dunbar A.D. 1650

Dunbar Law

Berwick

Northumberland

Durham

R. Tees

Westmorland

Cumberland

Lancashire

York

Lincoln

Derby

Cheshire

Flint

Denbigh

R. Trent

Dublin

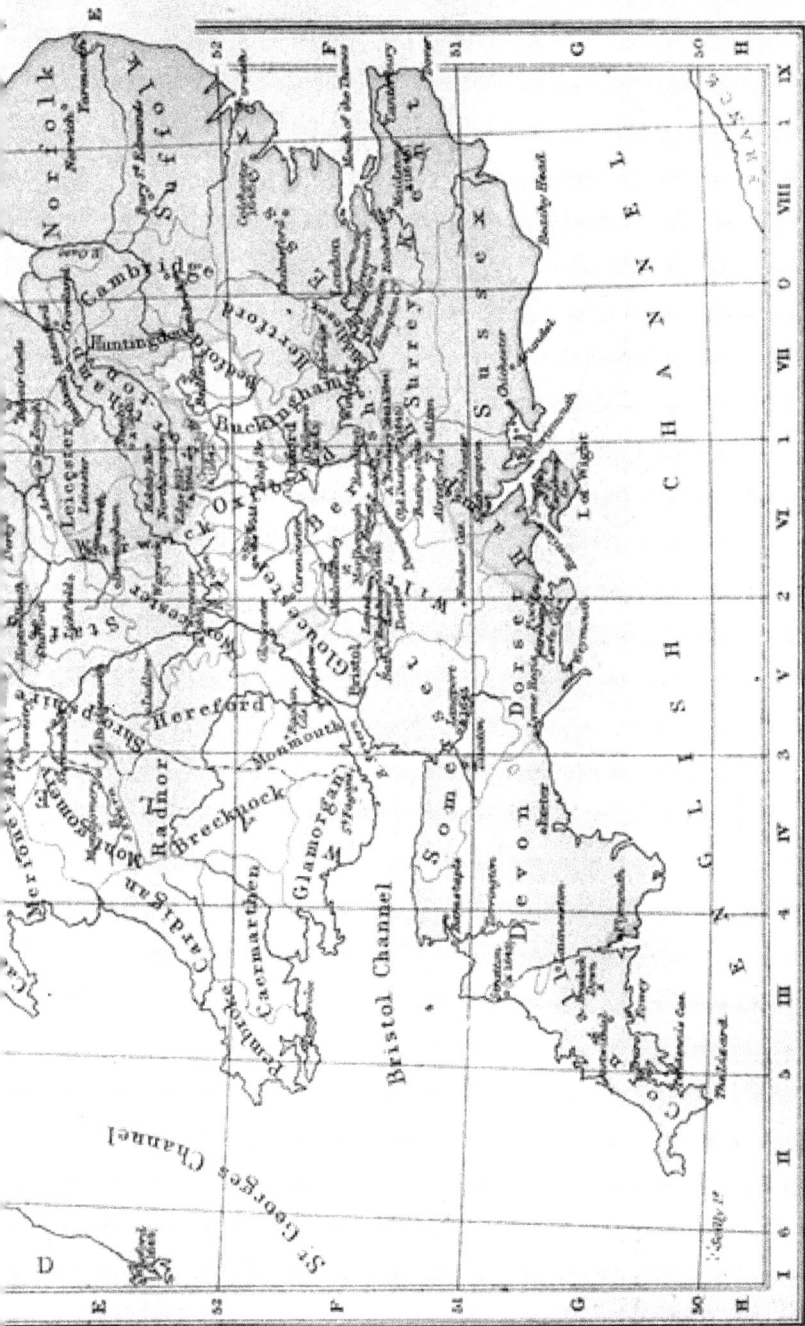

On the Parliamentary side Ferdinand, Lord Fairfax, commanded the right wing of horse, the first line consisting of English, the second of Scots; the centre was composed principally of Scottish infantry under old Alexander Leslie, Earl of Leven; the left wing of horse was commanded by Cromwell, his first line being composed of English, and the second of Scots under the leadership of David Leslie.

With extraordinary rashness and folly Rupert led his army down close to the enemy and posted it within striking distance, trusting that a ditch which covered his front would suffice to protect him from attack. The two forces having gazed at each other during the whole afternoon without moving, he at last dismounted between half-past six and seven and called for his supper, an example which was followed by several of his officers. The Parliamentary army seized the moment to advance with its whole line to the attack. Cromwell on the left led his cavalry across the ditch, and, though Rupert was quickly in the saddle to meet him, routed the leading squadrons of the Royalists.

Rupert's supports however were well in hand, and falling on Cromwell threw his troops into disorder [4] till David Leslie, an excellent officer, brought up the Parliamentary supports in their turn and routed the Royalists. Then superior discipline told; Cromwell's men quickly rallied and the whole of Rupert's horse fled away in disorder. In the centre the Parliamentary infantry was for a time equally successful, but the horse on the right wing came to utter disaster. The ground on the right was unfavourable for cavalry, being broken up by patches of gorse; and although Thomas Fairfax with a small body of four hundred men, armed with lances, broke through the enemy and rode in disorder right round the rear of the Royalist army, the main body was hopelessly beaten. Goring, after the Swedish fashion, had dotted bodies of musketeers among his horse, who did their work admirably.

Part of Goring's troopers galloped off first to pursue, and then to plunder the baggage, while the remainder turned against the Scotch infantry and pressed them so hard that, in spite of Leven's efforts, almost every battalion was broken and dispersed. Three alone behaved magnificently and stood firm, till in the nick of time Cromwell returned from the left to rescue them. His appearance turned the scale,

---

4. All kinds of reasons have been advanced to account for the (supposed) extraordinary fact that Cromwell's troopers at one moment were at a disadvantage. The explanation is quite simple, being no more than the usual swing of the pendulum in a combat of cavalry.

and the victory of the Parliament was made certain and complete.

Rupert after the action gave Cromwell the name of Ironside; he had never encountered so tough an adversary before. Marston Moor may indeed be termed the first great day of the English cavalry. We find, curiously enough, examples of three different schools in the field, the old school of the lance under Thomas Fairfax, the Swedish of mixed horse and musketeers under Goring, and the new English of Rupert and Cromwell; but the greatest of these is Cromwell's. He alone had his men under perfect control, and had trained them not only to charge, but what is far more difficult, to rally.

Little more than a week later came the first sign of an entirely new departure in the Parliament's conduct of the war. In spite of Marston Moor the general position of its affairs was anything but favourable. The inefficiency of local committees and the narrow self-seeking of local forces, combined with the jealousy of rival commanders and the absence of a commander-in-chief, threatened to bring swift and sudden dissolution to the cause. Time had aggravated rather than diminished the evil, and unless it were remedied forthwith, it would be useless to continue the war. Sir William Waller, an able commander, who had frequently suffered defeat less from his own incapacity than from the impossibility of keeping a force together, gave the authorities plainly to understand that unless they formed a distinct permanent army of their own, properly organised, properly disciplined, and regularly paid they could not hope for success.

Mutiny, desertion, and indiscipline had dogged every step of the local levies, as the Parliament very well knew; but experience still more bitter was needed before it could be induced to take Waller's advice. For the present it voted the formation of an army of ten thousand foot and three thousand horse and ordered it to be ready to march in eight days. Ignorance and infatuation could hardly go further than this. Shortly after came a great disaster in the west, nothing less than the capitulation of Essex's whole army. Then came the second battle of Newbury, which left the king in a decidedly improved position. Finally at the close of the campaign the Parliamentary forces sank into a condition which was nothing short of deplorable, the dissensions among the commanders rose to a dangerous height, and as a crowning symptom of the general collapse the Eastern Association, the strongest of all the local bodies, declared that its burden was heavier than it could bear and threw itself upon the Parliament. In the face of such a crisis the Houses could hesitate no longer, and on the 23rd of November they made over the whole state of the forces to the Committee of Both Kingdoms, with directions to consider a frame or model of the whole militia.

Thus the work that should have been done years before by Elizabeth was at length taken in hand; and the broken-down machinery of the Plantagenets was at last to be superseded. There was of course jealousy as to the hands in which so powerful an engine should be placed, and the difficulty was overcome only by the Self-denying Ordinance, which debarred members of both Houses of Parliament from command, and laid the ablest soldier in England aside as impartially as inefficient peers like Manchester and Essex.

But such an evil as this could be easily remedied, for something more than an ordinance is required at such times to exclude the ablest man from the highest post. To bring the New Model into being was the first and greatest task; and this was done by the Ordinance of the 15th of February 1645. The time was come, and England had at last a regular, and as was soon to be seen, a standing army.

Chapter 3

The Organisation of the Army

Even before the Ordinance for the establishment of the New Model Army had been passed, Parliament had voted, on the motion of Oliver Cromwell, that the chief command should be given to Sir Thomas Fairfax. There is little difficulty in discovering the reason for this choice. If by the Self-denying Ordinance all members of both Houses were to be excluded from command in order to rid the country of incompetent officers, there could be no doubt that Fairfax was the man best fitted to be captain-general. He had been the soul of the Parliamentary cause in the north, and, though by no means uniformly successful in the field, had shown vigour in victory, constancy in defeat, and energy at all times. Though not comparable to Cromwell in military ability, and perhaps hardly equal either to Rupert on the one side or to George Monk on the other, he was none the less a good soldier and a gallant man, though if anything rather too fond of fighting with his own hand when he should have been directing the hands of others.

He knew the value of discipline and was strong enough to enforce it, but he understood also the art of leading men as well as driving them to obedience. Heir of a noble family and born to high station, he could fill a great position with naturalness and ease; being above all things a gentleman, honourable, straightforward, disinterested, and abounding in good sense, he could occupy it without provoking envy or jealousy. No higher praise can be given to Fairfax than that every one was not only contented but pleased to serve under him.

Joined with him as sergeant-major-general, and therefore not only as commander of the foot but as chief of the staff, was the veteran Philip Skippon. His long experience of war in the Low Countries, and the respect which such experience commanded, doubtless

THE
BATTLE OF ABERDEEN

Covenanting Army ▢
Montrose's Army ■

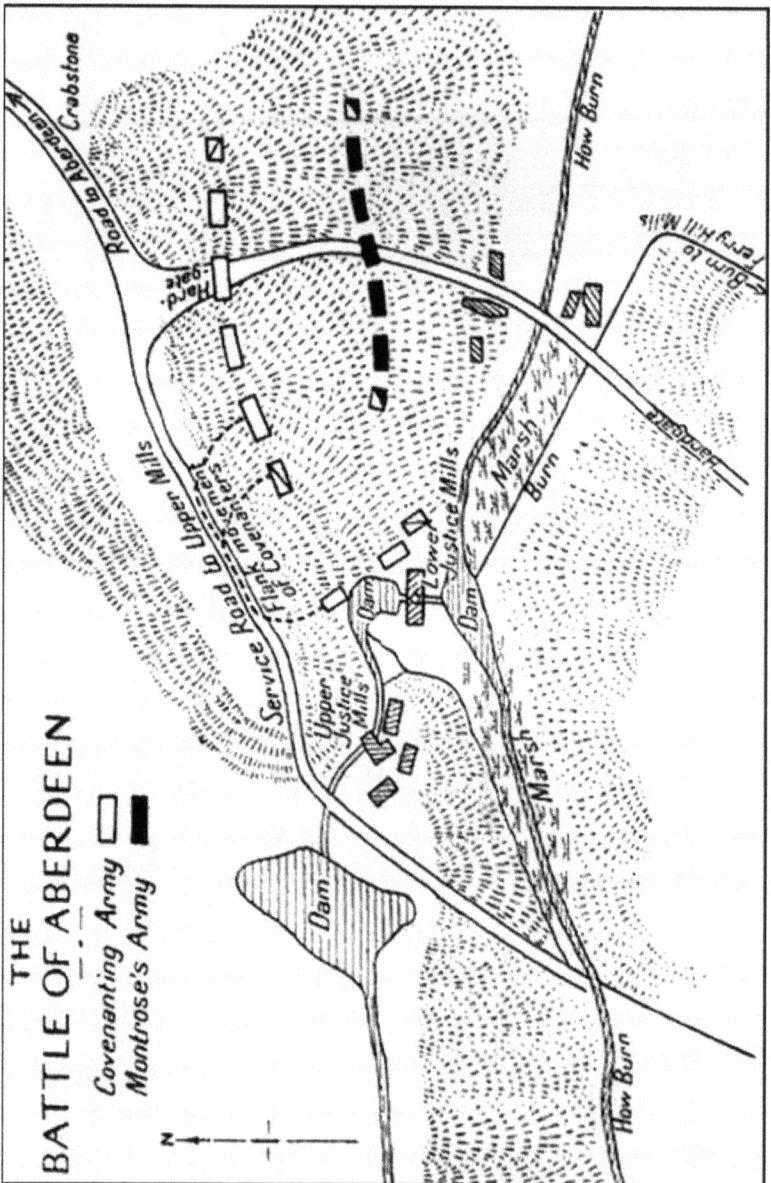

N

How Burn

Road to Aberdeen Crabstone

Hard-gate

Burn to Ferry Hill Mills

How Burn

Service Road to Upper Mills

Flank march of the Covenanters

Upper Justice Mills

Lower Justice Mills

Dam

Dam

Dam

Dam

Marsh Burn

Marsh

How Burn

prompted his selection to be Fairfax's chief adviser. The post of lieutenant-general, which carried with it the command of the cavalry, was left unfilled. Everyone knew who was the right man for the place, and there could be little doubt but that, notwithstanding all self-denying ordinances, he must sooner or later be summoned to hold it. For the present he was employed, pending the expiration of the forty days of grace allowed him by the Ordinance, in watching the movements of the Royalist forces in the west. Though there had been trouble even with his famous regiments in the general collapse at the close of 1644, yet it was noticed that in January 1645 no troops had appeared so full in numbers, so well armed, and so civil in their carriage as Colonel Cromwell's horse. One newspaper said:

> Call them Independents or what you will, you will find that they will make Sir Thomas Fairfax a regiment of a thousand as brave and gallant horse as any in England.

This however was not to happen at once. Fairfax, having obtained the Parliament's approval of his list of officers, was busily engaged with Skippon in hewing rougher material than Cromwell's troopers into shape. Many of the disbanded regiments of Essex lay ready to his hand, but they had lately shown a mutinous spirit which it required all Skippon's tact and firmness to curb. The old man, however, as he was affectionately called, knew how to manage soldiers, and the promise of regular pay, notwithstanding that one quarter of the same was deferred as security against desertion, soon brought them cheerfully into the service. Nevertheless there were, even so, not voluntary recruits enough to supply the twenty-two thousand men required by the Ordinance; more than eight thousand were still wanting, and the Committee of Both Kingdoms could think of no better means for raising them than the press-gang. This was the system which, when enforced by Charles the First, had been denounced as an intolerable grievance, and it was not less violently resisted when sanctioned by Parliament. The Government, however, carried matters with a strong hand, and a couple of executions soon brought the recalcitrant recruits to submission.

The scene of the making of the New Army which was destined to subdue the king was, by the irony of fate, royal Windsor. It is on the broad expanse of Windsor Park and on the green meadows by the Thames, before the wondering eyes of the Eton boys, that we must picture the daily parade of the new regiments, the exercise of pike and musket and the assiduous doubling of ranks and files, old Skippon, gray and scarred with wounds, riding from company to company and instituting mental comparisons between them and the English soldiers of the Low Countries, and the younger sprightlier Fairfax, still but three-and-thirty, watching with all a Yorkshireman's love of horseflesh the arrival of troopers and baggage-animals. Every day the scene grew brighter as corps after corps received its new clothing, for the whole army, for the first time in English history, was clad in the familiar scarlet. Facings of the colonel's colours distinguished regiment from regiment; and the senior corps of foot, being the general's own, wore his facings of blue. [1] Thus the royal colours, as we now call them, were first seen at the head of a rebel army.

The senior regiment of horse was also in due time to be clothed in the same scarlet and blue. For Cromwell's two regiments of horse had been selected, as was their due, to be blent into one and to take precedence, as Sir Thomas Fairfax's, of the whole of the English cavalry. In this same month of April the regiment was in the field, turning out quicker than any other corps on the sounding of the alarm, while the "lovely company" of which the colonel had boasted, now called the general's troop, was distinguishing itself above all others. Modern regiments of cavalry that wear the royal colours need not be ashamed to remember that they perpetuate the dress of Oliver Cromwell's troopers. Excluded though Cromwell was from the making of the New Model Army, he was none the less its creator, for it was he who had shown the way to discipline and regimental pride.

It is now necessary briefly to sketch the organisation of the New Model. Beginning therefore with the infantry, the foot consisted of twelve regiments, each divided into ten companies of one hundred and twenty men apiece. As all the field-officers, even if they held the rank of general, had companies of their own, the full number of officers to a regiment was thirty: colonel, lieutenant-colonel, major, seven captains, ten lieutenants and ten ensigns. Each company included moreover two sergeants, three corporals, and one, if not two, drums. [2]

The privates were divided as usual into an equal number of pikemen and musketeers: the weapons of officers being, for a captain, a

---

1. *Perfect Passages,* 30th April 1645.
2. The drum-calls were six in all: 1, Call; 2, March; 3, Troop; 4, Preparative; 5, Battle; 6, Retreat. The trumpet-calls were also six: 1, *Butte sella,* corrupted since into "Boot and Saddle"; 2, *Monte cavallo* (mount); 3, *Tucket* (warning' for march); 4, *Carga* (charge); 5, *Alia Standarda* (to the Standard); 6, *Auquet* (watch-setting).—Ward, *Animadversions of Warre.*

pike; for a lieutenant, the partisan; and for an ensign, the sword. Since Skippon, a veteran of the Dutch school, was at the head of the infantry, it can hardly be doubted that the Dutch system of drill was preferred to the Swedish. Gustavus Adolphus, it must be remembered, was chiefly concerned with the Scots; while the contemporary drill books of the English prefer the teaching of Maurice of Nassau. It is therefore reasonably safe to conclude that the normal formation of the infantry of the New Model was not less than eight ranks in depth.

The cavalry consisted of eleven regiments, each of which contained six troops of one hundred men. Here again every field-officer had a troop of his own, so that the full complement of officers to a regiment numbered eighteen, namely, colonel, major, four captains, six lieutenants, and six cornets. Three corporals and a trumpeter were included among the hundred men; and the admirable system which sorted each troop into three divisions, each under special charge of an officer and a corporal, was in full working order. In the matter of drill and tactics, the English cavalry was before rather than behind the times. The modified shock-action of Gustavus Adolphus had, under the influence of Rupert and Cromwell, been virtually superseded. The men indeed were still armed, according to the old fashion, with iron helmet and cuirass, and still carried each a brace of pistols as well as a sword; but they were instructed to trust to their swords in the charge, and to use their fire-arms only in the pursuit.

Gustavus had formed his horse as a rule in four ranks; Rupert fixed the depth at three;[3] the Parliamentary officers went so far as to reduce the ranks to two, sacrificing depth to frontage, and trusting to speed, we cannot doubt, to overcome weight. Last and most daring innovation of all, they abolished the file as the tactical unit of the troop and substituted the rank in its place.[4] No better testimony to the improvement of English discipline could be found than this reduction in the depth of the ranks of cavalry. For once it may be said that the English horse stood in advance of all Europe.

As regards the duties of reconnaissance, not a treatise on cavalry omits to mention that it is the function of the horse to scour the ways in advance of an army; but there are no precise directions as to the

---

3. *The Young Horseman and Honest Plain-dealing Cavalier*, by John Vernon, 1644. A short drill-book in pamphlet form, prepared by a cavalier-officer in small compass for officers "to weare in their pocket." This is the first soldier's pocket-book for field service in our language. It is among the King's Pamphlets in the British Museum.
4. Barriffe.

manner of fulfilling it. Cromwell's constant references to a "forlorn" of horse show that he employed advanced parties regularly, and attention has already been called to the efficiency of Rupert's patrols. There is no evidence, however, that the men received any instruction in the matter of reconnaissance, and it is only from the Royalist Vernon that we learn that vedettes were posted then, as now, in pairs.

The dragoons of the New Model seem, in spite of a resolution of the Commons that they should be regimented, to have been organised in ten companies, each one hundred strong. Their officers were a colonel, a major, eight captains, ten lieutenants, and ten ensigns. The dragoons were mounted infantry pure and simple, riding for the sake of swifter mobility only, and provided with inferior horses. They were armed with the musket and drilled like their brethren of the foot; their junior subalterns were called ensigns and not cornets, and they obeyed not the trumpet but the drum. Their normal formation was in ten ranks of ten men abreast. For action, nine out of the ten dismounted, and linking their horses by the simple method of throwing the bridle of each over the head of his neighbour in the ranks, left them in charge of the tenth man. [5]

Next we must glance at the Artillery which, together with the transport, was comprehended under the head of the Train. The only organised force of which we hear as attached to the train is two regiments of infantry and two companies of firelocks, which were used for purposes of escort only. The firelocks were distinguished from the rest of the army by wearing tawny instead of scarlet coats, and seem therefore to have been a peculiar people, but the immediate connection of flint-lock muskets with cannon is not apparent.

The truth seems to be that the English were behind the times in respect of field artillery, and indeed we hear little of guns, except siege-cannon, during the whole period of the Civil War. English military writers of the period rarely make much of artillery in a pitched battle. They recommend indeed that the enemy's guns should be captured by a rush as early as possible, and they generally agree that cannon should be posted on an eminence, since a ball travels with greater force downhill than uphill. On the other hand, it was objected even to this simple rule that if guns were pointed downhill there was al-

---

5. Sometimes however the dragoons seem to have taken with them ten extra men per company simply to hold the horses. There are fugitive references to light dragoons even at this early period, but no clear account of them. After a few years it was as usual to speak of troops as of companies of dragoons.

ways the risk of the shot rolling out of the muzzle, so that in truth the gunner seems to have been sadly destitute of fixed principles for his guidance in action.

The neglect of field artillery in England is the more remarkable inasmuch as English gun-founders enjoyed a high reputation in Europe. The cannon of that day were necessarily heavy and cumbrous, since the bad quality and slow combustion of the powder made great length imperative; but there was no excuse for not imitating the light field-pieces of Gustavus Adolphus. The probable reason for the backwardness of the English was the peculiar organisation of the Dutch artillery, which gave no opening for the instruction of English gunners in the school of the Low Countries. Nevertheless there was a distinct drill for the working of guns, with thirteen words of command for the wielding of ladle and sponge and rammer. A gun's crew consisted of three men—the gunner, his mate, often called a matross, and an odd man who gave general assistance; and the number of little refinements that are enjoined upon them show that the artillerymen took abundant pride in themselves. Thus the withdrawal of the least quantity of powder with the ladle after loading was esteemed a "foul fault for a gunner to commit," while the spilling even of a few grains on the ground was severely reprobated, "it being a thing uncomely for a gunner to trample powder under his feet."

Lastly, every gunner was exhorted to:

Set forth himself with as comely a posture and grace as he can possibly; for the agility and comely carriage of a man in handling his ladle and sponge is such an outward action as doth give great content to the standers-by.

Nevertheless artillerymen seem nowhere, and least of all in England, to have been very popular. They had an evil reputation all over Europe for profane swearing, a failing which is attributed by one writer to their enforced commerce with infernal substances, but which was more probably due to the fact that, being less perfectly organised than other branches of the army, they were less amenable to rigid discipline.

But if the gunners were but a casual and ill-administered force, much more so were the drivers. Over a thousand draught-horses were collected for the general use of the New Model, but how many, if any, of these were set apart for the artillery, it is impossible to say. Ordinary waggoners with their teams were impressed or hired to haul the guns, and it is recorded that the hackney-coachmen of London performed the duty more than once. The chief use of the escort of infantry was therefore to prevent the drivers from running away. It is doubtful whether the guns themselves travelled on four wheels or on two, contemporary drawings showing instances of both; but in either case there was no approach to what is now called the limber, the horses being harnessed simply to the trail. [6]

The ammunition again was transported in ordinary waggons, the powder being indeed occasionally made up into cartridges, but more often carried simply in barrels which were unloaded behind the gun when it was posted for action. It was the function of the odd man of the gun's crew to cover up the powder-barrel between each discharge of the gun, to avert the danger of a general explosion. In fact, one principal link alone connects the artillery of the New Model with the artillery of today, (1899), the gun-carriages were painted of a fair lead-colour.

Lastly we come to the Engineers, a corps which is more obscure to us even than the Artillery. Even in the days of the Plantagenets the English kings had taken Cornish miners with them for their sieges; and in the war of Dutch Independence Yorkshire colliers were specially employed for the digging of mines. But, although by the middle of the sixteenth century the Germans had already organised a corps of sappers, [7] no such thing existed in England. In truth, the British were not fond of the spade. The English indeed handled it often enough under Vere and his successors, while the Scots, though sorely against the grain, were forced to do the like by Gustavus Adolphus. But considering the schools wherein the British were trained, nothing is more remarkable in the Civil War than the neglect of field-fortification and the extreme inefficiency with which at any rate the earlier sieges were conducted. It is significant that the pioneers, [8] who are the only men that we hear of in connection with the unorganised corps of engineers, were the very scum of the army, and that degradation to be "an abject pioneer" was a regular punishment for hardened offenders. It is still more significant that the principal engineers of the New Model Army bear not English but foreign names.

So much for the various branches of the military service: it remains to say a few words of the army as a whole. Of the organisation of what

---

6. Which was then called the limber.

7. Schanzbauern. *Fronsperger.*

8. They stood on much the same level in France.

would now be called the War Department, it is extremely difficult to speak. There was a parliamentary Committee of the Army, which seems to have enjoyed at first an intermittent and later a continuous existence, and which was entrusted with the general direction of its affairs and in particular with the business of recruiting. There were also Treasurers at War, who were charged with the financial administration, and there was the already venerable Office of Ordnance, which was responsible for arms and equipment. Speaking generally, though the functions of the committee and of the treasurers seemed to have overlapped each other at various points, the military administration seems to have tended to the following allocation of responsibility: that the Committee of the Army took charge of the men, the Office of Ordnance of the weapons and stores, and the Treasurers at War of the finance, while the Commander-In-Chief was answerable for the discipline of the army.

Passing next to purely military organisation, which of course fell within the province of the Lord-General, it is to be remarked that the makers and commanders of the New Model knew of no better distribution of command than under the three heads of Infantry, Cavalry, and Train. There was no such thing as a division comprehending a proportion of all three arms under the control of a divisional commander; and though we do hear frequently of brigades, the word signifies merely the temporary grouping of certain corps under a single officer, rarely an essential part of the general organisation. The subjoined list gives a tolerable idea of the allotment of functions among the members of the staff. It is only necessary to add that all orders of the commander-in-chief were issued through the sergeant-major-general, distributed by him to the sergeant-majors or, as they are now called, majors of the different regiments, and by the sergeant-majors in their turn to the sergeants of every company and the corporals of every troop.

Commander-in-Chief.
His Excellency Sir Thomas Fairfax, Knight, Captain-General.
Headquarter Staff.
(Chief of the Staff)—Major-General [9] Skippon.
Commissary-General of the Musters.—Comm.-Gen. Stone
(with two deputies).
Commissary-General of Victuals.—Comm.-Gen. Orpin.
Commissary-General of Horse Provisions.—Comm.-Gen.

9. So in Sprigge, more properly Sergeant-Major-General.

Cooke.
(Transport} Waggon-Master-General.—Master Richardson.
(Intelligence) Scout-Master-General.—Major Watson.
(Military Chest) Eight Treasurers at War (civilians), (with one
deputy).
Judge Advocate-General.—John Mills (civilian).
(Medical) Physicians to the Army.—Doctors Payne and
Strawhill.
„ Apothecary to the Army.—Master Web.
Chaplain to the Army.—Master Boles.
(Military Secretary) Secretary to the Council of War.—
Mr. John Rushworth (civilian), with two clerks.
(*Aides-de-Camp*) Messengers to the Army.—Mr. Richard
Chadwell, Mr. Constantine Heath.

Foot. [10]

Major-General	Skippon
Quartermaster-General	Spencer
Assistant-Quartermaster-General	Master Robert Wolsey.
Adjutant-General	Lieut.-Colonel Gray.
Marshal-General	Captain Wykes.

Ten regiments of foot; each regiment of ten companies; each
company of one hundred and twenty men, exclusive of the
officers

REGIMENT.	COLONEL.	REGIMENT.	COLONEL.
1st.	{ Sir Thomas Fairfax. { Lieut.-Colonel Jackson.	5th.	Harley.
2nd.	{ Major-General Skippon. { Lieut.-Colonel Frances.	6th.	Montague.
		7th.	Lloyd.
3rd.	Sir Hardress Waller.	8th.	Pickering.
4th.	Hammond.	9th.	Fortescue.
		10th.	Farringdon.

Horse

Lieutenant-General	Oliver Cromwell.
Commissary-General	Henry Ireton.
Quartermaster-General	Fincher.
Adjutants-General	Captains Fleming and Evelyn,
Marshal-General	Captain Laurence.

10. In Sprigge's list the foot take precedence of the horse; and this was the rule in
the English, though not in the French, Army.

Mark-Master General   Mr. Francis Child.

Eleven regiments of horse; each of six troops; each troop of one

REGIMENT.	COLONEL.	REGIMENT.	COLONEL.
1st. {	Sir Thomas Fairfax. Major Disbrowe.	6th.	Lieut.-General Cromwell.
2nd.	Butler.	7th.	Rich.
3rd.	Sheffield.	8th.	Sir Robert Pye.
4th.	Fleetwood.	9th.	Whalley.
5th.	Rossiter.	10th.	Graves.
		11th.	Comm.-General Ireton.

The captain-general's bodyguard consisted of one troop, taken from his regiment of horse, under Colonel Doyley.

Dragoons.

Colonel Okey.

Ten companies each of one hundred men, besides officers.

Train.

Lieut.-Gen. of the Ordnance	Lieut.-General Hammond.
Controller of the Ordnance	Captain Deane.
Engineer General	Peter Manteau van Dalem
Engineer Extraordinary	Captain Hooper.
Chief Engineer	Eval Tercene.
Engineers	Master Lyon, Master Tomlinson..
Master Gunner of the Field	Francis Furin
Captain of Pioneers	Captain Cheese.

A Commissary of Ammunition.

A Commissary of the Draught Horses.

Two Regiments of Infantry	Colonel Rainborough's. Colonel Weldon's

Two companies of Firelocks.

The regiments of the New Model were not yet complete when Fairfax received orders from the Committee of Both Kingdoms to march westward to the relief of Taunton. It is extraordinary that this presumptuous body of civilians, even after it had provided the general with an efficient army, still took upon itself to direct the plan of campaign. It is still more extraordinary that Fairfax, who had disregarded it before Marston Moor, should now have meekly obeyed. Charles, whose chief hopes rested in a junction with the gallant and victorious

Montrose, was actually moving northward to meet him while Fairfax was tramping away to Taunton. Nay, even after Taunton had been relieved, the sage Committee could think of no better employment for the New Model than to set it down to the siege of Oxford. Fatuity could hardly go further than this. There were in the field on both sides four armies in all, ranged alternately, so to speak, in layers from north to south. Northernmost of all was Montrose, below him in Yorkshire lay Leven with the Scots, south of Leven was Charles, and south of Charles the New Model. And yet the Committee proposed to keep Fairfax inactive before Oxford while Charles and Montrose crushed Leven between hammer and anvil.

A brilliant victory of Montrose at Auldearn (May 9), brought matters to a crisis. Leven was compelled to retreat into Westmoreland; and the Scots insisted that Fairfax must break up from before Oxford and move up towards the king. Charles, meanwhile, with his usual indecision had suspended his march northward for the sake of capturing Leicester, and was now lying at Daventry, uncertain whither to go next. Fairfax called a council of war, which decided to seek out the enemy and fight him wherever he could be found, and, more important still, requested the appointment of Cromwell to the vacant post of lieutenant-general.

The Parliament meanwhile had come to its senses, and resolved that the general should henceforth conduct his own campaign without the advice of a committee of civilians. Having done so, it could hardly refuse to sanction the return of Cromwell. He was therefore summoned to headquarters; and Fairfax began to work in earnest. So energetic were his movements, when once the paralysing hand of the Committee was withdrawn, that the Royalists at once jumped to the conclusion that "Ironside" had rejoined the army.

He had not yet rejoined it, and yet the Royalists were right, for it was his spirit, the spirit of discipline, that was abroad in the army. The New Model was by no means perfect when it marched from Windsor at the end of April 1645. The old failings of insubordination, desertion, and plunder, natural enough among a body of men largely recruited by impressment, showed themselves abundantly at the outset of the march to Oxford, but they were put down with a strong hand, not by preaching, but by hanging. Nor was it by severity only that Fairfax brought men to their duty.

According to custom, every regiment was told off in succession to furnish the rearguard, but when the turn of Fairfax's regiment came,

Boath House

Castle Hill

MACDONALD

HURRY

2 2 2

2 2 2

2 2 2

Church

Auldearn

Boggy
Ground

A

MONTROSE

N

THE
BATTLE of AULDEARN

Montrose ...... ▨
Hurry .... □
Scattered Troops ·····

Hill marked A now covered with wood
and known as Deadman's Wood

0   ⅛   ¼   ½
Scale of Half a Mile

the men claimed that, being the general's own, they had a right to a permanent place in the van. Fairfax said nothing, but simply jumped off his horse and tramped along in the midst of them in the rearguard; and after this there were no more quarrels over precedence. After a month in the field the newspapers could report that oaths, quarrelling and drunkenness were unknown in the New Model. "Yea, but let Cromwell be called back," they added; and before long this too was done.

CHAPTER 4

Naseby

At six o'clock on the morning of the 13th of June, while Fairfax was sitting at a council of war, Cromwell marched into the camp at Kislingbury at the head of his regiment. It was but a small reinforcement of six hundred troopers, but as they rode in a cheer rose from the cavalry which was taken up by the whole army, as the word ran round the camp that Noll was come. Next day was fought the Battle of Naseby. It was not a well-managed fight. After considerable shifting of position, so much prolonged that Rupert came to the conclusion that Fairfax wished to decline an engagement, the New Model Army was finally drawn up on the plateau of a ridge about a mile to the northeast of Naseby village. It lay behind the brow of a hill which slopes down somewhat steeply to a valley below called the Broadmoor, and was formed according to the usual fashion of the time.

Six regiments of three thousand six hundred horse formed the right wing, seven thousand infantry under Skippon made up the centre, two thousand four hundred more horse under Ireton made the left. Ireton's flank was covered by a hedge, which by Cromwell's direction was lined with dismounted dragoons. The disposition of the Royalists was of the same kind, though their force was of little more than half the strength of the New Model. The right wing of cavalry was under Rupert, the centre of infantry under old Sir Jacob Astley, the left wing of cavalry under Sir Marmaduke Langdale. Each army held two or three regiments of infantry in reserve.

Rupert, conspicuous in a red cloak, opened the action by a rapid advance with his horse against Fairfax's left. Ireton thereupon drew over the brow of the hill to meet him, and Rupert, evidently rather astonished to find so large a force in front of him, incontinently halted. Ireton then made the fatal mistake of halting likewise. Whether he was

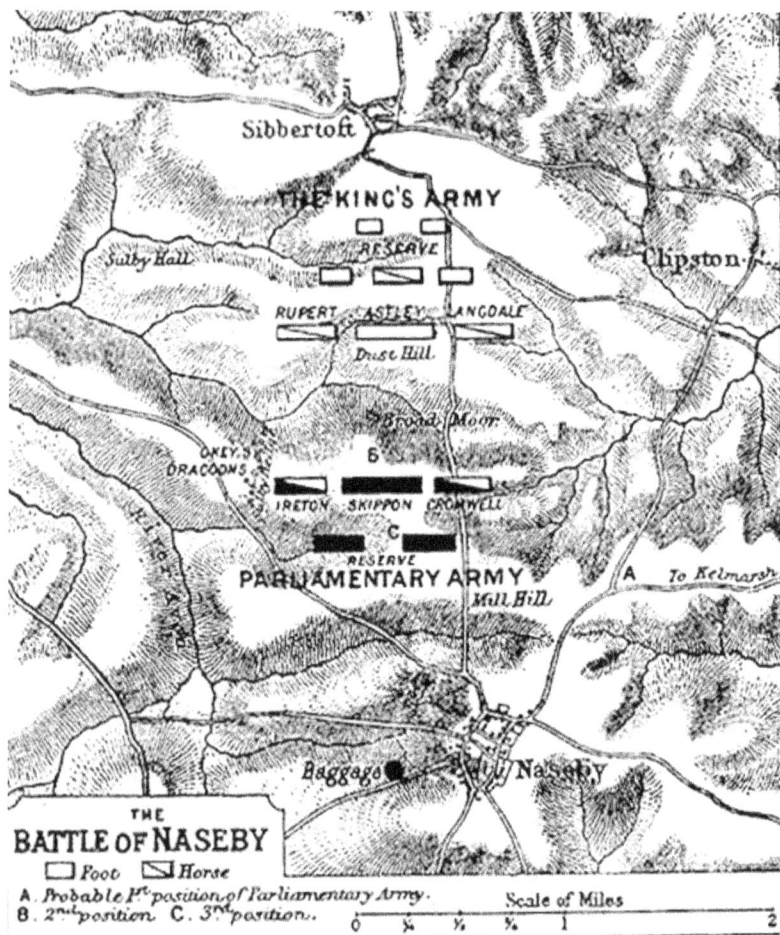

Sibbertoft

THE KING'S ARMY

Sulby Hall

RESERVE

Clipston

RUPERT   ASTLEY   LANGDALE

Dust Hill.

Broad Moor

OKEY'S
DRAGOONS

IRETON   SKIPPON   CROMWELL

C

RESERVE

PARLIAMENTARY ARMY

Mill Hill.

A   To Kelmarsh

Baggage

Naseby

THE
BATTLE OF NASEBY

☐ Foot   ▱ Horse

A. Probable 1ˢᵗ position of Parliamentary Army.
B. 2ⁿᵈ position C. 3ʳᵈ position.

Scale of Miles

0   ¼   ½   ¾   1   2

hampered by the ground or unequal to the task of handling so large a body of horse, is uncertain; but, whatever the reason, his wing was in disorder, and instead of continuing the advance he began to correct his dispositions. Rupert at once seized the moment to attack. A few divisions under Ireton's immediate leadership charged gallantly enough and held their own until driven back by Rupert's supports, but the rest hung back, and Rupert pressing on, as was his wont, scattered them in confusion.

Ireton, losing his head, instead of trying to rally them, plunged down with his few squadrons on the Royalist infantry, was beaten back, wounded and taken prisoner; and in fact the left wing of the New Model was for the time completely overthrown. Away went Rupert in hot pursuit with his troopers at his heels for a mile beyond the battlefield, and galloping up to the park of Parliamentary baggage, summoned it to surrender. He was answered by a volley of musketry, and then too late he recollected himself and rode back to the true scene of action.

In the centre also matters again had gone ill with the Parliament. Skippon was wounded early in the day, and though he refused to leave the field was unable actively to direct the engagement. Either his dispositions were incomplete, or his colonels were helpless without him; but the left centre, its flank exposed by Ireton's defeat, gave way and in spite of all the efforts of the officers could not be rallied. Fortunately Fairfax's regiment on the right centre stood firm; and the steadiness of three regiments in the reserve enabled the Parliamentary infantry to maintain the struggle.

But it was on the right that the best soldier in the field was stationed, and his presence counted for very much. He too was hampered by bad ground, patches of gorse and a rabbit-warren on his extreme right preventing all possibility of a general advance of his wing. But instead of halting like Ireton he took the initiative in attack. The leftmost troops under Whalley, having good ground before them, at once moved down, fired their pistols at close range, [1] and fell in with the sword. Langdale's horse met them gallantly enough, but were beaten back and retired in rear of the king's reserve, where they rallied. But Whalley's supports came up quickly to second him, and meanwhile the rest of Cromwell's wing came up as best it could over the broken ground, and falling on the opposing bodies of Royalist horse routed all in succession.

---

1. This incident shows that shock-action was not yet wholly the rule.

The Royalists retreated for a quarter of a mile and rallied; and Cromwell, detaching part of his horse to watch them, rode down with three regiments against the king's reserve of horse. Charles, to do him justice, bore himself gallantly enough, but some one gave the unlucky word, "To the right turn—march!" whereupon the whole of his men turned tail and sweeping the king along with them joined their beaten comrades in rear. Thither also presently came Rupert with such a following of blown and beaten horses as he could collect. Ireton's wing had rallied, and was pressing so close on his rear that he dared not stop; and Rupert's foolish and premature pursuit had squandered his squadrons as effectually as a defeat.

The whole of Charles's army was now beaten or dispersed except his centre, and against this the whole force of the Parliamentary army was now directed. Okey, who commanded the dragoons, finding the ground clear before him, made his men mount and attacked it in flank; Fairfax's regiment of foot engaged it in front, and Ireton's rallied troopers in rear. All soon laid down their arms excepting a single battalion, [2] which stood alone with incredible courage and resolution till it was fairly overwhelmed. Even so, however, Fairfax dared not advance further till he had reformed his whole line of battle.

But the Royalists could not face a second attack; they turned and fled; and the Parliament's cavalry pursued the fugitives for fourteen miles, capturing the whole of the king's artillery, his baggage, and practically his entire army. It was a decisive victory though not a very glorious one. But for Cromwell, who alone after Skippon's fall seems to have kept his wits about him and his men in hand, Naseby would probably have added one more to the indecisive battles of the Civil War.

Nevertheless the New Model had won its first action, and Fairfax now started on a campaign to the west, which did not end until he had penetrated through Somerset, Devon, and Cornwall, and crushed Royalism under foot even to the Land's End. It was a long march of incessant and at first of severe fighting, which taxed the mettle even of his best soldiers, but the army gathered strength, in spite of constant hardships, in its swift progress from victory to victory, and by the summer of 1646 it had finished the work begun at Naseby and was virtually master of England.

Meanwhile the persistent folly of the king had raised it from a par-

2. Called by the name of a *tercio* in the contemporary plans, being formed probably in the old Spanish formation which Tilly had used at Leipsic.

tisan to a national army. Charles, who had no spark of patriotic feeling in him, had from the first striven not only to set nationality against nationality within the British Isles, but had appealed to foreigners from France, Lorraine, and Holland to uphold his rights. All these transactions had been revealed by the capture of his baggage at Naseby; and his defiance of all the insular prejudice of the English damaged him unspeakably even with those who were most sincerely attached to his cause. Margaret of Anjou was not yet forgotten; and if men coupled Charles's name with hers, it was no more than he deserved.

Now, however, he was beaten, beaten on every side. In the first six months of 1645 Montrose, perhaps the most brilliant natural military genius disclosed by the Civil War, had scored success after success with a handful of Scots and Irish. A woman in emotion and instability, a man in courage, and a magician in leadership, he was an ideal leader for such untameable, combative spirits, the stuff of which Dundonalds are made. Yet Montrose's work had been undone at Philiphaugh, and Charles's last hope was gone. A few more ineffectual struggles to divide England against herself, and he was to be purged away as a public enemy by the ever victorious army.

NORTH SEA

CAMPAIGN of PHILIPHAUGH

Montrose's March ————
Leslie's March ‑ ‑ ‑ ‑

0 5 10 15 20 25 30
English Miles

CHAPTER 5

The Cruellest Necessity

On the subjugation of the west the English Parliament thought for the present only of securing its position within England itself. It has been seen how at the first outbreak of the war the Parliamentary leaders had taken the Scottish Army into pay, and how even after the formation of the New Model they had tried to saddle it with the hardest of the work. In truth, the behaviour of the Parliament towards the Scots had been sufficiently shifty and ungracious; it had taken at any rate some care to pay its own troops, but it persistently neglected its allies, who had done excellent service in the north. Indeed, had Leven yielded to the English Parliament's wishes, had he not in fact been forced by the victory at Auldearn to retreat, the Scots instead of the English might have won the Naseby of the Civil War, an event which would have led to untold complications.

Now however that the English Army had done the work for itself, all parties in England became anxious to be rid of the Scots. Matters were somewhat confused by the fact that in Charles threw himself into the hands of Scotland; but by the close of the year it was agreed that the Scottish army should be paid off and withdrawn over the border, and that the king should be surrendered to the English, who had conquered him. The Parliament therefore gained its great object, a free hand for the management of its own affairs. It overlooked however in its calculations one important factor, the army.

At the opening of 1647 there was a general cry throughout England for peace. The country was exhausted; the finance of the Parliament was in hopeless disorder; and the people groaned under the enormous expense of the war. Obviously the most natural item for retrenchment was the army; its work was done, and there was no further reason for its existence; it should therefore be disbanded or at any rate very greatly reduced. Moreover economy was not the only motive that prompted such a policy. The Parliament, united for the moment in the general desire to get quit of the Scots, fell back, almost immediately after this was accomplished, into faction. Presbyterians and Independents were the original names of the two rival parties, but for our purpose it is simpler to narrow them forthwith to Parliament and Army; for among many of the Presbyterian members who had held commands in the first years of the war, there existed a professional as well as a political and religious jealousy of the successful officers who had supplanted them. Parliament having created the army by a vote thought that it could extinguish it by the same simple process; having used it as a ladder whereon to rise to undisputed supremacy it now proposed to kick it down. But such an army was not disposed to make itself a plaything of Parliament.

Petitions from various quarters for the disbandment of the New Model turned the heads rather than strengthened the hands of the two Houses. The only safe and honest course, if the army must be disbanded, was to discharge the whole of the country's obligations to it in full. Now the pay of the foot was eighteen weeks and of the horse forty-two weeks in arrear, and the total debt due to the forces amounted to three hundred and thirty thousand pounds. The Parliament was in straits for money and by no means inclined to make the necessary effort to raise this sum.

It proposed as an alternative to turn twelve thousand of the soldiers into a new army for the pacification of Ireland, and this without a word as to the terms on which the men had taken service, and without the least mention of a settlement of arrears. Further, as if it were not enough to irritate the men, the Parliament did its best to alienate the officers. It passed resolutions insulting to the army, insulting to Fairfax, insulting to Cromwell. So deeply injured indeed was Oliver by this ungrateful treatment, that he thought seriously of carrying his sword and such troops as he could raise to the wars in Germany. Such was the pitch of disgust to which the Parliament had driven the ablest of its servants.

The army raised its first protest in the form of a respectful petition from the men: the Parliament met it with violent and ungracious censure. Certain officers who had supported this petition then tendered a vindication of their conduct: the Commons refused even to read it. Finally, as if to aggravate the army to extremity, the Lords proposed to grant the troops six weeks' pay in temporary satisfaction of arrears. This was too much. Discontent grew apace in the ranks, the men refused to have anything to do with service in Ireland, and finally the Army, by the election of two representatives for each regiment, organised itself for the orderly maintenance of its just claims. These representatives were called agitators, a name which in those days signified simply agents. The degradation of the term in our own time into a synonym for political busybodies must not mislead us, nor blind us to the dignified patience, under extreme provocation, of this irresistible body of disciplined men.

For the moment the Parliament was awed into concessions and promises, but its leaders did not lightly submit to humiliation, and rather than yield to the army looked about for a force to countervail it. First they turned to the City of London, which was strongly Presbyterian, and sought an armed force in the City train-bands. Next they resorted to Scotland, which was intensely jealous of the New Model, and formed a coalition with it in favour of the king, thereby sowing the seeds of a quarrel between North and South Britain. Finally, after stultifying itself by a promise of attention to the army's complaints, it passed an Ordinance for its disbandment without further ado.

This was past endurance. The soldiers broke into open mutiny; and Fairfax and Cromwell, having striven in vain to gain justice for their men, and at the same time to keep them in subordination to the Parliament, placed themselves at the head of a movement which they could no longer repress. It was indeed high time, for the Presbyterian leaders had already invited the Prince of Wales to place himself at the head of the Scots for an invasion of England.

On the 4th of June the army assembled about four miles from Newmarket at Kentford Heath. There in the course of the next few days it erected a general council, composed of the general officers who had taken the side of the men and of two officers and two privates from each regiment, and made a written declaration of its policy. Still the Parliament remained obstinate, and now endeavoured to enlist the discharged soldiers of the earlier armies in order to meet force with force. The army advanced to Triplow Heath, whither Parliament sent a last message to propose terms for an agreement. The overtures were rejected, and the army continued its advance.

In panic fear the Parliament now offered bribes to any officers or men who would desert the army. This contemptible device was a total failure. It then tried to raise troops, to reopen negotiations with the army, to call out the London trained bands, to forbid the army's further advance, to gain certain troops, which were not of the New Model, from the north; all was in vain. Irresistible as fate, the army marched on. At St. Albans it halted and issued a manifesto demanding the expulsion of eleven of its enemies from the Commons, and receiving no encouragement advanced to Uxbridge. There again it halted and spent three weeks in the hopeless effort to arrange a peaceful settlement with the king; and finally it marched straight into London, (August 6), and occupied the capital.

Still the Commons persevered in opposition to the army; and at last Cromwell, without the orders and in spite of the unwillingness of Fairfax, gave the Presbyterian majority a strong hint to convert itself into a minority. His arguments consisted of one regiment of horse, stationed in Hyde Park, and a small party of foot at the door of the House; and they were sufficient and conclusive. The House thus purged, Cromwell turned to the task which was to occupy the remainder of his life and drive him worn-out to his grave, a final settlement of the original quarrel. Wisely enough he thought that this could be effected only by agreement with the king; and it was to negotiation with Charles Stuart for this object that he now devoted the whole of his energy.

But negotiation with a man who was constitutionally incapable of straightforward and honourable dealing could have but one end. The lower ranks of the army, not more far-seeing but less sanguine than their leader, again interposed. A section of extremists, known at that time by the name of Levellers, began, as is usual at such times, to raise its head, and condemning all further traffic with the king boldly put forward a revolutionary scheme of its own.

Herein, however, the Levellers mistook their man. However Cromwell might be distracted by the difficult questions of a settlement, he was perfectly clear on one point, that the discipline of the army must be maintained. Symptoms all too significant appeared that that discipline was impaired, and he lost no time in restoring it. One regiment refusing to obey his orders, Cromwell promptly drew his sword and rode single-handed straight into the middle of the malcontents. His resolution speedily convinced the men that he would not be trifled with; the mutineers yielded, and a single execution sufficed to re-establish order.

January, 1648, as usual the portentous folly of the king united all parties not only in the army but in England against himself. He might have made honourable terms with Cromwell; he preferred to throw

himself into the arms of the Scots. Both Houses of Parliament thereupon broke with their North British allies, and the dispute assumed
the new phase of a quarrel between English and Scots. English refugees inflamed national feeling at Edinburgh, and on the nth of April
the Scottish Parliament pronounced the treaty between the two nations to be broken. By the first week in May the army which was to
invade England began slowly to assemble, and on the 8th of July it
crossed the border, ten thousand five hundred strong, and occupied
Carlisle.

Meanwhile the energies of the English had been distracted by Royalist risings in Kent and in Wales which kept Fairfax and Cromwell
both busily employed; and it was not till the 11th of July that Cromwell
was able to leave Pembroke and march to the north. Even then his
force, after a trying campaign in very inclement weather, was in no
very good state. He was entirely destitute of artillery, and his men
were most of them both shoeless and stockingless. In one principal
respect, however, the force was strong, for it was perfect in spirit and
in discipline. I shall not dwell on the details of Cromwell's dash from
Wales into Yorkshire.

The Scots, embarrassed by a multitude of commanders, suffered
him to attack their far more numerous army in detail, when it was
divided on opposite banks of the Ribble; and after one sharp engagement at Preston the campaign resolved itself into a mere pursuit of
the beaten Scots. How hotly Cromwell pressed the chase, and with
what hardships to his own little army, may be read in his own despatches. Unfavourable weather, torrents of rain, and the miserable state
of the roads brought men and horses to the last stage of exhaustion.
Cromwell wrote:

> The Scots are so tired and in such confusion that if my horse
> could but trot after them we could take them all, but we are so
> weary we can scarce be able to do more than walk after them .
> . . . . my horse are miserably beaten out, and we have ten thou-
> sand prisoners.

The memory of this swift raid into Yorkshire, and of the unrelent-
ing chase that followed it should be treasured by the British cavalry
that fought through the Pindarri war and the Central Indian campaign of 1857-58.

With the close of the pursuit after Preston, the second Civil War
came to an end. The operations of Fairfax in the south had shown

him at his very best, swift, active, and resolute, and had been brilliantly successful. Those of Cromwell in the north, though they were directed against Royalist Scotland only, not yet the sterner Scotland of the Covenant, had been crushing. England was now completely under the sway of the Parliament; but it became a question whether Parliament was its own master. A movement arose in the army for the punishment of the men who had brought all this bloodshed upon the country, and in particular of the chief delinquent, Charles Stuart, who was guiltiest of all. By a final overture for a settlement the army gave the king a last chance, and on its failure appealed to Parliament to bring him to justice.

Ireton seems to have been the moving spirit in the actions that followed, though there can be no doubt that Cromwell was in full sympathy with them. Oliver was intensely English in spirit, and had been greatly exasperated by the English Royalists who had called the Scots over the border. He was vehement for justice upon them, and upon the King as the chief of them. Parliament, on the other hand, was engaged in nominal negotiations with Charles; and it was therefore not to be expected that it would comply with the army's request that he should be brought to trial. But the army was not to be stopped. The king's person was seized; the Parliament was purged of recalcitrant members; and from these actions to the High Court of Justice the march was short.

One leading soldier, Fairfax, did indeed recoil from the final step, but the majority of the officers pressed on; and on the 30th of January 1649, the king was brought out into the ring of red coats to meet his death. He had done his worst against the British Isles. He had invited foreign armies against England, and when he failed had roused Welsh, Scots, and Irish to a hopeless effort to subdue her. But he succeeded only in establishing her strength; and the fall of his head was but the first instalment of the great work done by Cromwell and the army towards the unity of the islands under the supremacy of England.

We have a pleasant glimpse of Oliver in his lighter moods before he next unsheathed his sword. On the evening of the 23rd of February, as he and Ireton were returning from dinner with Bulstrode Whitelocke, their coach was stopped by the soldiers who were in charge of the streets. They explained who they were, but the captain of the guard would not believe them and threatened to put them into the guard-room. Ireton began to lose his temper, but Cromwell laughed, and pulling out twenty shillings gave them to the men as a reward for doing their duty. Less than three weeks later he was summoned to take command of the army that was collecting for the reconquest of Ireland; for that unlucky island had been chosen by the Royalists as the base of operations for the invasion of England.

CHAPTER 6

Ireland & Scotland

Rupert, now turned admiral, had already sailed to Kinsale to enlist Irish sailors, and the faithful Ormonde had invited Charles the Second to place himself at the head of the loyal party in Ireland. Cromwell was not unwilling to undertake the duty. He had no idea of yielding England either to Scots or Irish, least of all to the Irish, whose land was regarded rather as a colony than as an integral part of the realm, and was also a stronghold of papistry. Still he declined to accept the command until he had assured himself that all the wants of his troops should be satisfied; he loved his men and would not suffer them to be enticed by the magic of his name to thankless or unprofitable service.

Four regiments of foot and one of horse were then chosen by lot, and the men were informed that they need not go to Ireland unless they wished, but that if they refused they would be discharged from the army. Several hundred men thereupon at once threw down their arms and were dismissed; but by some blunder, which was none of Cromwell's, not a word was said about the payment of the arrears that were due to them.

The idea spread through the ranks that they must either go to Ireland or forfeit those arrears; discontent was naturally aroused and presently burst out into formidable mutiny.

Fairfax and Cromwell, however, could depend on their own regiments, and faced the danger with extraordinary swiftness and energy. The mutineers were suppressed with a strong hand. One ringleader was executed in St. Paul's Churchyard, a cornet and a corporal were shot before the eyes of their comrades against the walls of Burford Church, and discipline was again restored.

Shortly after, Parliament passed an Ordinance to relieve the financial difficulties of the soldiers, and the preparations for the Irish campaign were resumed. It is curious to note the extreme slowness with which the civilians learned that soldiers were after all men of flesh and blood, not puppets to be hugged or broken according to the caprice of the hour.

The details of the preparations for the war in Ireland may still be read in the State Papers of the time. There are still to be seen the orders for fifteen thousand cassocks, "Venice-red colour, shrunk in water," the like number of pairs of breeches "of grey or other good colour," ten thousand shirts, ten thousand hats and bands, [1] one thousand iron griddles, fifteen hundred kettles, giving a curious picture of the equipment of the first English regular army for what was then esteemed to be foreign service. But I shall not follow the red coats through the terrible Irish campaign of 1649. It was not, like the later war with the Scots, an honourable contest for supremacy: it was rather the stern suppression of a rebellion, wherein the spirit of the masters was inflamed by the insolence of long superiority, by the bitterness of religious hatred, and by the recollection of past outrages which, even if truly reported, would have kindled men to vengeance, and when exaggerated by rage and fear fairly blinded them to mercy.

If any Englishman doubted whether the Irish could fight with desperate gallantry he was undeceived at the storm of Drogheda and at Clonmel: but they could not stand, untrained and unorganised as they were, against the veterans of the New Model. Much has been said about Cromwell's cruelty, and that he was ruthlessly severe there can be no question; but when we speak of cruelty we should take at any rate some account of the standard of humanity in the warfare of the seventeenth century. The Irish War was a war of races, a war of creeds, and a war of vengeance. That there should therefore have been such slaughter as at Drogheda and at Wexford is nothing surprising, [2] however deplorable.

What is really remarkable in such a war is that Cromwell, from the moment of landing, should have paid his way, visited plunder with the sharpest penalties, and upheld the sternest and most inflexible discipline. Forty years later, when the conquest of Ireland was undertaken by a former marshal of France and a king long schooled in war against

---

1. This item furnishes indirect evidence that either few pikemen were employed, or that if employed they were stripped of defensive armour. The pike was already falling obsolete.

2. See the very pertinent extract from Wellington's despatches, quoted by Mr. Gardiner—*Commonwealth*, vol. I.

the first generals of the time, they were glad to search out Cromwell's plans for his Irish campaign and follow them at such a distance as they might.

Cromwell was still in full career of victory, (January 8), when the alarming news of a treaty between Charles the Second and the Scots moved the Parliament to recall him to watch over its own safety. He arrived in London on the 1st of June, and was joyfully welcomed not only by Fairfax and the officers of the army but by all ranks and all classes. It was now almost certain that the Scots would invade England in the king's name, and no time was lost by the Council of State in appointing Fairfax and Cromwell to command the English Army in the north. That they would work loyally together in the field no one could doubt; but when the Council consulted the two generals as to plan of campaign, their opinions were found to be diametrically opposed to each other.

Cromwell was for taking the bull by the horns and carrying the war into Scotland before the Scots could cross the border; Fairfax, never quite at his ease since the establishment of the Commonwealth, thought such aggressive action unjustifiable. It is impossible to believe that this was his true military opinion, but not all the arguments of the Council nor the pressing entreaty of Cromwell could prevail with him to alter it. Despite all protests he resigned his commission on the plea of physical infirmity, and from this moment passes out of the history of the army. Never perhaps has that army possessed a more popular and deservedly popular commander-in-chief.

Only one man could be his successor. On the selfsame 26th of June Cromwell received his commission as captain-general and commander-in-chief; and two days later he started on his journey to the north. Charles Fleetwood was his lieutenant-general, John Lambert, an excellent soldier, his major-general; and joined to his staff was another officer whom we saw fighting in the Low Countries many years ago, Colonel George Monk. He had served in the Civil War first with the Royalists, and had been taken prisoner by Fairfax at Nantwich in January 1645; he had then passed some time in confinement in the Tower, and finally had taken service with the Parliament in Ireland, where his merit had attracted the attention of Cromwell.

Oliver was now anxious to provide him with a regiment; but the corps which he had designed for him was unwilling to receive a Royalist for colonel. Five companies were therefore taken from Sir Arthur Hazelrigg's regiment at Newcastle and as many more from Colonel

Fenwick's at Berwick; and the ten companies were united into Monk's regiment of foot. Thus was formed the oldest of our existing national regiments, the one complete relic of the famous New Model,[3] the one surviving corps which fought under Oliver Cromwell, itself more famous under its later name of the Coldstream Guards.

On the 19th of July Cromwell halted near Berwick, where he mustered sixteen thousand men, a third of them cavalry; and on the 22nd he crossed the Tweed and marched up the coast upon Edinburgh. A fleet on the east coast provided him with supplies as he advanced, which furnishes an interesting precedent for the system that was to be seen later under Wellington in the Peninsula. On the 28th of July he was at Musselburgh, and on the following morning he came in sight of the Scottish Army, which was entrenched along the line from Leith to the Canongate.

The Scottish force comprehended a nominal total of twenty-six thousand men, of which eighteen thousand were foot and eight thousand horse. It was under the command, in deed if not in name, of David Leslie, the same excellent officer who had routed the brilliant Montrose at Philiphaugh and had handled his cavalry so efficiently at Marston Moor. His troops however were inferior in quality to the English. It is true that in 1647 the Scotch had followed the example of England in remodelling their army, but the total strength of this force was but five thousand foot and fifteen hundred horse; and this, even supposing the whole of it to have been efficient, was but a small leaven among twenty-six thousand men. Leslie therefore stood carefully on the defensive and resisted all Cromwell's temptations to a pitched battle.

After a couple of days Cromwell was compelled to fall back to Musselburgh for supplies. He then determined to march round Edinburgh and push on to Queensferry, where he could regain touch with his fleet on the northern side of the town. Political reasons however induced him to linger in the execution of this project, and the delay enabled Leslie to take up a position which rendered it impossible. Unable to force Leslie to an engagement, and not daring to attack him with inferior numbers, Cromwell found himself completely outmanoeuvred. Dysentery broke out in the English troops; supplies began to fail; and he was compelled to fall back by Haddington and Mus-

---

3. The pedigree of Monk's regiment is as follows: Weldon's Regiment of the New Model became first Robert Lilburn's, and in 1649-50 Sir A. Hazelrigg's. Lloyd's of the New Model passed in succession to Herbert, Overton, and in 1649 to Fenwick.

selburgh to his ships at Dunbar.

There he arrived on the 1st of September with "a poor, shattered, hungry, discouraged army." The Scots had pressed the pursuit very closely, the rearguard had been constantly engaged, and, most significant of all, the English discipline even under Oliver himself had begun to fail. [4] Having driven his enemy into the peninsula of Dunbar, Leslie sent forward a force to bar a defile on the road to Berwick at Cockburnspath, and cut off his retreat. The situation of the English was desperate, and Cromwell was at his wits' end. His army was reduced by sickness to eleven thousand men, while the Scots still numbered twenty-three thousand; he could expect no relief from Berwick; and Leslie lay in a strong position, from which it was hopeless to attempt to dislodge him, between him and the Tweed.

Leslie on his side might well feel confident that he held his enemy in the hollow of his hand. He had but to remain on his hill-side and watch the English army melt away, or wait for the most favourable moment to attack it either in the effort to embark or while struggling through the defile in retreat. He was however not his own master, but was controlled by an Aulic Council called the Committee of Estates, which urged him to descend from his weather-beaten position on the hill and move to the ground below, where he would not only find greater convenience of supplies but stand within closer striking distance of his enemy.

Down therefore he came, not altogether unwillingly, and took up a new position on a triangle of ground enclosed between the sea, the hill which he had just left, and a small stream called the Broxburn. This stream, which runs at the bottom of a course from forty to fifty feet deep, covered the whole of his front. On his extreme left it runs close under the steep declivity of the hill and forms with it, so to speak, the apex of the triangle; but further down it quits the slope and takes its own course to the sea, leaving plenty of space between it and the hill for a camping-ground.

Halfway between the open space and the sea, by the grounds of Broxmouth House, the deep banks of the stream give place, as is usual with such waters, to gentle inclines, not unfavourable to the action of cavalry. This point by Broxmouth House formed Leslie's extreme right. The whole position, as he judged, was not ill suited to a force with great superiority in cavalry. He could post his foot on his centre and on his left behind the deep trench dug by the Broxburn, and mass

4. Hodgson.

his horse on the right where it could dash down the gradual incline and across the shallow water without risk or difficulty. By four o'clock in the afternoon of the 2nd of September his new dispositions were complete.

Cromwell from the other side of the stream followed every movement with intense attention. At last turning to Lambert he said that he thought the enemy gave him an opportunity. Lambert replied that the very same idea had occurred to him. Monk, who had probably received higher military training than any officer in the army, was next appealed to, and cordially agreed. If Leslie's right, at the base of the triangle, could be turned, the whole of his force must be pent up between the hills and the burn, his horse hurled on to the backs of his foot, and the entire army forced up to the gorge at the apex of the triangle in ever increasing confusion, and, in a word, lost. The time of attack was fixed for the morrow before dawn, and the details of the English dispositions were entrusted to Lambert.

Rain fell in torrents all through the night, and the Scotch picquets laid themselves down to sleep with what comfort they could among the corn-shocks. The English, as ever even during the worst and most disorderly of retreats, had recovered themselves at the prospect of battle. At four the moon rose and found Lambert already hard at work. The bulk of the force, six out of eight regiments of horse and three and a half regiments of foot, was moved down to the extreme English left. Five regiments of horse under Lambert were to cross the burn by Broxmouth House and attack the Scottish cavalry in front; three regiments of foot and one of horse, all picked corps, were to cross the water farther down and sweep round upon its right flank. Cromwell himself took command of this turning movement, and the regiment of horse which he took with him was that which he had made six years before on the model of his own " lovely company." The remainder of the force with the artillery was stationed along the edge of the trench of the Broxburn to check any movement of the enemy's centre and left.

The light was beginning to creep over the sea before Lambert had posted the artillery to his liking. There was some stir in the Scotch camp; a trumpet sounded *boute-selle*; and Cromwell, fearful lest the enemy should gain time to change position, grew impatient for Lambert's coming. At last he came, and both columns moved off. Lambert's regiments of horse advanced to the burn; and then the trumpets rang out, and the troopers dashed across the water and poured up the op-

BATTLE OF DUNBAR.
3RD Sept.r 1650

MAP IX

FIRTH OF FORTH

Dunbar

From Edinburgh.

A ⬜ ⎡Brocksmouth H.

Broxby

B

THE BROCKSBURN

to Berwick

CROMWELL'S ARMY . . . A
SCOTTISH " . B
TURNING MOVEMENT →

Lammermoor Hill

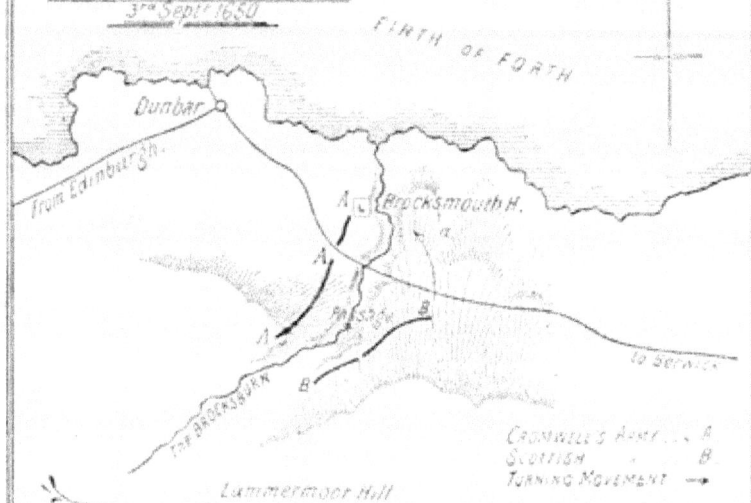

GENERAL MAP of PART of SCOTLAND .

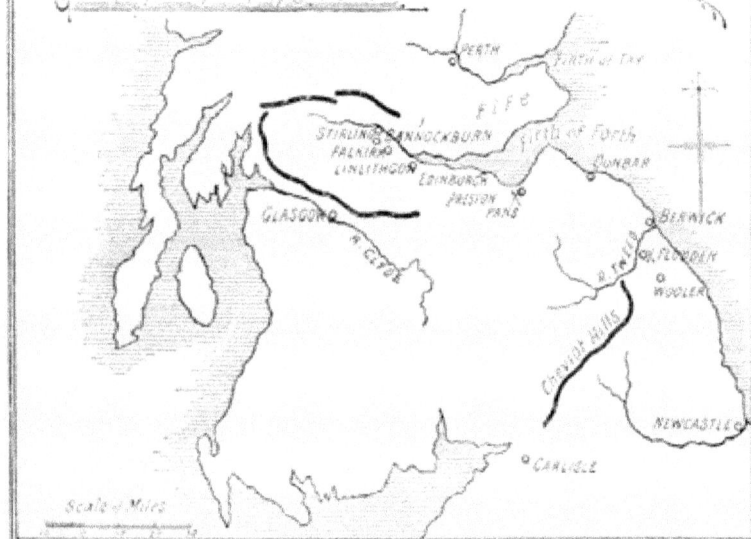

PERTH

FIRTH of TAY

FIFE

STIRLING BANNOCKBURN
FALKIRK
LINLITHGOW

FIRTH of FORTH

EDINBURGH

PRESTON
PANS

DUNBAR

GLASGOW R. CLYDE

BERWICK

R. TWEED
R. FLODDEN
WOOLER

CHEVIOT HILLS

NEWCASTLE

CARLISLE

Scale of Miles

posite slope to the attack. The Scots, though unprepared, met them gallantly enough. Foreigners would have called them ill-equipped, for they carried lances, an obsolete weapon, in their front rank; but the lance was in place in the shock-combat which Cromwell had taught to the English cavalry, and the first onset of the English horse was borne back across the burn. The supports came quickly up and the fight was renewed, though against heavy odds, for the Scots could bring infantry and guns to the aid of their horse, which the English could not yet.

But while the combat of cavalry was still swaying to and fro, the infantry of Cromwell's turning column came up steady and inexorable upon the flank of the Scots. Still Leslie's gallant men fought on for a short time undismayed. They had been faultily disposed, as Cromwell had noted, and could not easily change front,[5] but they met the new attack as best they might and even checked the leading regiment of English infantry. But Cromwell's own regiment of foot came up in support, strode grimly forward straight to push of pike, and swept the stoutest corps of Scottish infantry into rout.

Then the Scots lost heart and wavered; the English, horse and foot, gathered themselves up for a final terrible charge; and the Scottish cavalry, reeling back upon the foot, carried it away in choking disorder towards the gorge. Meanwhile Cromwell was urging his third regiment of foot to the left, always farther to the left; and as, panting and breathless, they climbed the lower slopes of the hill they saw the whole length of the battle spread out before them and the Scotch all in confusion. "They run, I profess, they run!" cried Oliver as he looked down. And while he spoke the sun leaped up over the sea, and flashed beneath the canopy of smoke on darting pikes and flickering blades and glancing *casques* and swaying *cuirasses*, as the redcoats rolled the broken waves of the Scottish Army before them.

"Now let God arise and let His enemies be scattered," cried Cromwell in exultation, for the victory was won. The Scots, wedged tighter and tighter between hills and stream, were caught like rats in a pit, and like rats they ran desperately and aimlessly up the steep slope, only to be caught or turned back by the English skirmishers above them. Their horse fled as best they could with the English cavalry spurring, broken ranks were reforming he sang the hundred and seventeenth Psalm, the chorus swelling louder and louder behind him as trooper after trooper fell into his place. Then the psalm gave way to the sharp word of com-

5. Hodgson.

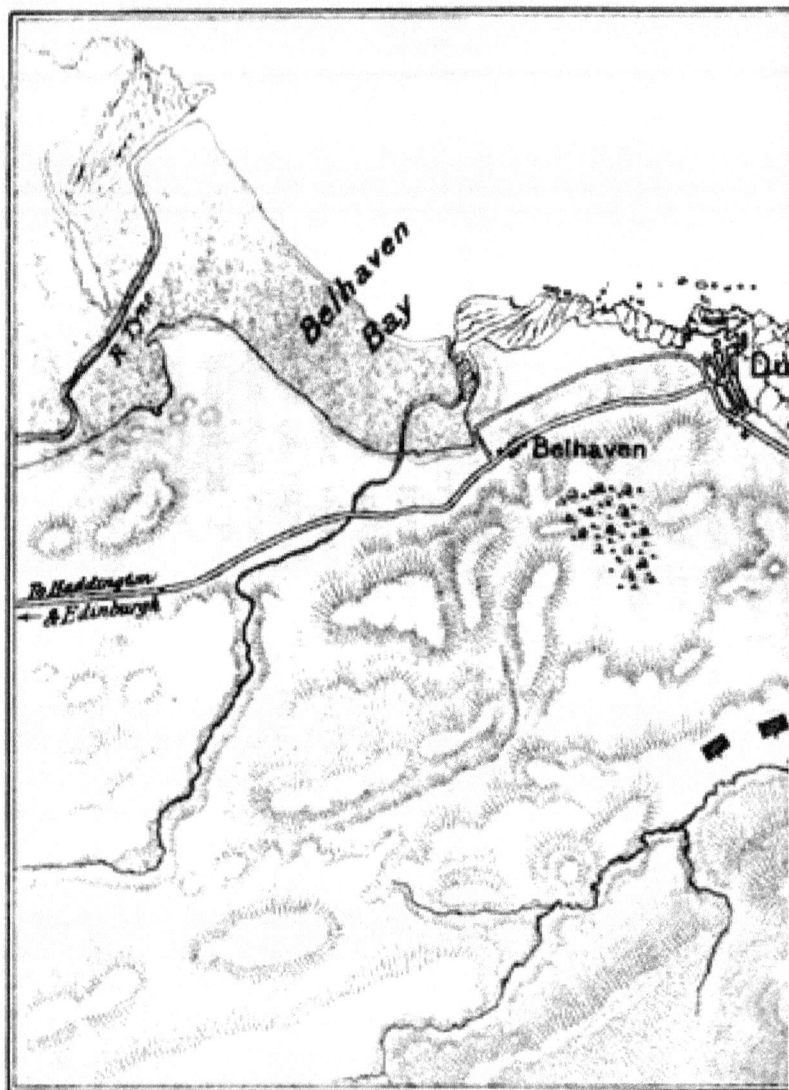

R. Dye

Belhaven Bay

Belhaven

To Haddington
& Edinburgh

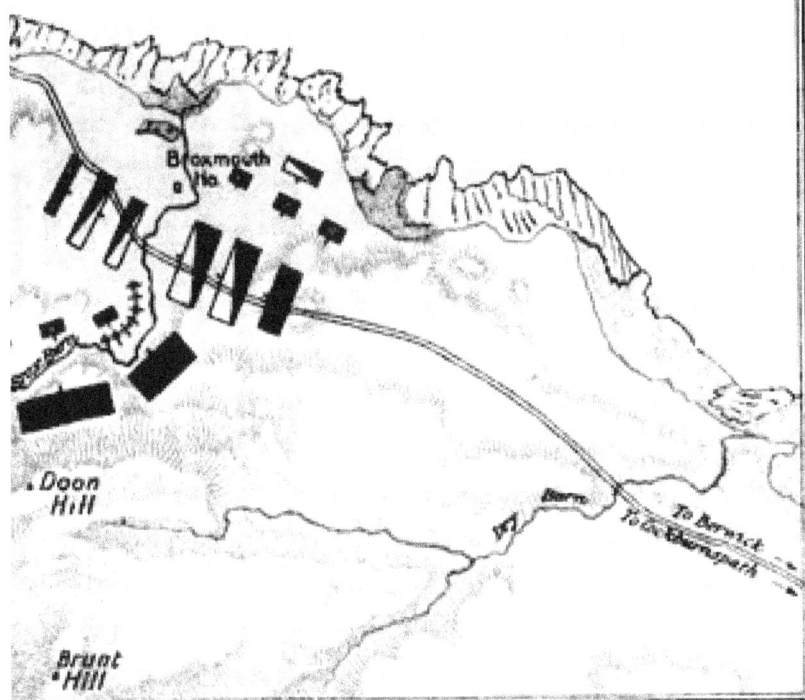

DUNBAR.

September 3rd 1650

Scale 1 inch = 1 mile

English ▬ *Scotch* ▬

nbar

Broxmouth Ho.

Doon Hill

To Berwick

Brunt Hill

mand, and the horse trotted away once more to the pursuit past Dunbar and Belhaven even to Haddington. Three thousand of the Scots fell in the field; ten thousand prisoners, with the whole of the artillery and baggage and two hundred colours, were taken. It was the greatest action fought by an English army since Agincourt.

Cromwell lost no time in following up his success. On the day after the battle he sent Lambert forward with six regiments of horse to Edinburgh, and occupied the port of Leith and the whole of the town, except the castle, without resistance. Leaving sufficient men to blockade the castle and hold the works at Leith he pushed on against Leslie, who had entrenched himself with five thousand men at Stirling; but finding his position unassailable he returned to Edinburgh and busied himself with the reduction of the castle, while Lambert completed the subjugation of the West. In the middle of September the castle surrendered, and therewith all Scotland south of the Forth and Clyde was subject to the English.

At Westminster the joy over the victory of Dunbar was enthusiastic, and found vent in the grant of a medal [6] and of a gratuity to every man who had fought in the campaign. This, the first medal ever issued to an English army, bore, in spite of his protests, the effigy of Cromwell upon the obverse, no unfitting memorial of the first founder of our army of today. But the struggle even now was not yet over. Royalist Scotland had been beaten at Preston, the Scotland of the Covenant at Dunbar; but Charles Stuart was able, by unscrupulous lying and shameless hypocrisy, to unite both for a last effort in his cause, and to gather a new army around that of David Leslie at Stirling. Accordingly on the 4th of February 1651 Cromwell left his winter-quarters for Stirling, but was compelled by the severity of the weather to retreat, with no further result to himself than a dangerous attack of fever and ague, which kept him on the sick-list until June.

On the 25th of June the English Army was concentrated on the Pentland Hills, and from thence marched once more to Stirling. Leslie, true to the tactics which had proved so successful in the previous year, had occupied an impregnable position which no temptation could induce him to quit. After a fortnight's manoeuvring, therefore, Cromwell decided, like Surrey before Flodden,[7] to move round Leslie's left flank

---

6. This again seems to be borrowed from the French. Vieilleville issued medals bearing the king's effigy to his troops in 1558, with a ribbon of his own colours (see *Memoires de Vieilleville*).

7. *The Battle of Flodden Field* by Robert Jones is also published by Leonaur.

and to cut off his supplies from the north. It is plain, from the fact that Monk had been engaged in operations for the reduction of Inchgarvie and Burntisland on the northern shore of the Firth of Forth, that Cromwell's plans for this movement were fully matured.

The first step was to send Lambert across the Firth with four thousand men to entrench himself at Queensferry. Leslie met this move by detaching a slightly inferior force against Lambert, which was utterly and disastrously routed, with a loss of five-sixths of its numbers. Ten days later Inchgarvie and Burntisland fell into Cromwell's hands, and, his new base being thus secured, he advanced quickly into Fife. Meanwhile he sent orders to General Harrison, whom he had left at Edinburgh with a reserve of three thousand horse, that he was to move at once to the English border in the event of Leslie's marching southward.

By the 2nd of August he had received the surrender of Perth, but, even before he could sign the capitulation, intelligence reached him that the Scots had quitted Stirling two days before and were pouring down to the border. Leaving five or six thousand men with Monk to reduce Stirling, he at once hurried off in pursuit.

Two days sufficed to bring his army to Edinburgh, where he halted for forty-eight hours. Harrison had already marched for the Border, and with ready intelligence had mounted some of his infantry to strengthen his little force. Lambert was now despatched with three thousand horse to hang upon the enemy's rear; a letter was despatched to the Speaker exhorting the Parliament to be of good heart; and on the 6th of August Cromwell resumed his advance. Both armies, English and Scots, were now fairly started on their race to the south. Charles, in the hope of picking up recruits, stuck to the western coast and the Welsh border, moving by Carlisle, Lancaster, and the ill-omened town of Preston. Cromwell's course lay farther east; he passed by Newburn, a scene of English defeat, and by the more famous field of Towton, where the south had first taught a lesson of respect to the north. Lambert and Harrison united, and on the 16th of August obtained contact with the enemy at Warrington, but not venturing to attack retired eastward to cover the London road and to draw closer to the line of Cromwell's march.

The Ribble and the Aire once passed, the two armies began to converge. On the 22nd of August Charles halted with the Scots at Worcester and proceeded to fortify the town, and four days later Cromwell occupied Evesham. Charles had but sixteen thousand men;

while Cromwell by a masterly concentration had collected no fewer than twenty-eight thousand. The militia, which had been reorganised by the Parliament in the previous year, had been called out and had answered admirably to the call. There could be little doubt of the issue of an action where the advantages both of numbers and of quality were all on one side, and there is no need to dwell on the battle fought on the anniversary, (September 3), of Dunbar at Worcester. It was a victory in its way as complete as Sedan: hardly a man of the Scottish army escaped. But it was also the crown of the great work of the army, the establishment of England's supremacy in the British Isles.

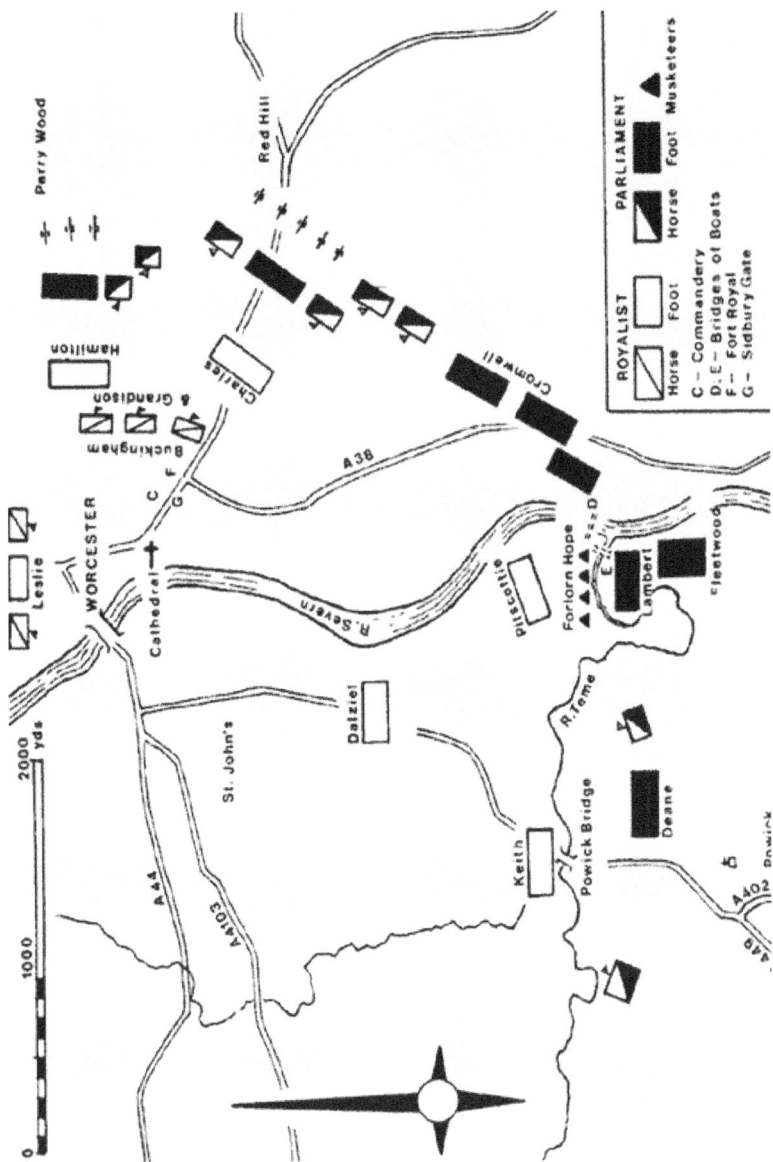

Parry Wood

Red Hill

Hamilton

& Grandison

Buckingham

Charles

WORCESTER

Leslie

Cathedral

A38

C

F

G

D

Forlorn Hope

Piscotia

R.Severn

Cromwell

Lambert

Fleetwood

St. John's

Dalziel

R.Teme

Deane

Keith

Powick Bridge

Powick

A44

A4O3

A402

A44

0   1000   2000 yds.

ROYALIST

Horse   Foot

C – Commandery
D, E – Bridges of Boats
F – Fort Royal
G – Sidbury Gate

PARLIAMENT

Horse   Foot   Musketeers

CHAPTER 7

Gradual Increase of the Army During the Civil Wars

The victory had not long been reported to Parliament when the House began to consider the question of reducing the forces. Silently and almost imperceptibly the strength of the Standing Army had grown since 1645 until it now amounted to thirty regiments of foot, eighteen of horse and one of dragoons, or close on fifty thousand men. Besides these there were independent companies in garrison to the number of seven thousand more, and several more regiments which were borne permanently on the Irish establishment. Five whole regiments, thirty independent companies, and two independent troops were ordered to be disbanded forthwith; other regiments were reserved for service in Ireland or to replace the disbanded companies in garrison; and the establishment for England and Scotland was fixed at eighteen regiments of foot and sixteen of horse. It appears too that the actual strength of companies was reduced from one hundred and twenty to eighty, and of troops from one hundred to sixty, thus diminishing the number of men while retaining the name of the corps intact. The system is no novelty in these days, but this is the first instance of its acceptance in the history of the army.

A revolutionary government, however, does not easily find peace. By June 1652 the recruiting officers were abroad again, and regiments were increasing their establishment owing to the outbreak of the Dutch War. The quarrel with the United Provinces was curious, inasmuch as the English commonwealth had expected sympathy from the sister-republic which had been made by English soldiers, and had even sought to unite the two republics into one. But there is no such thing as national gratitude; and the discourtesy of the Dutch soon

70

led the English to exchange friendly negotiations first for the Act of Navigation and very shortly after for war. The story of that war belongs to the naval history of England, wherein it forms one of its most glorious pages. Never perhaps has more desperate fighting been seen than in the six furious engagements which brought the Dutch to their knees.

Yet in these too the redcoats to the number of some two thousand[1] took part, under the command of men who had made their mark as military officers—Robert Blake, Richard Deane and, not least, George Monk. The last named was so utterly ignorant of all naval matters that he gave his orders in military language—"Wheel to the right," "Charge"—but he made up for all shortcomings by his coolness and determination. When Deane, his better-skilled colleague, was cut in two by a round shot at his side he simply whipped his cloak over the mangled body and went on fighting his ship as though nothing had happened. Finally, in the last action of the war he boldly met the greatest admiral of the day, and one of the finest sailors of all time, with but ninety ships against one hundred and forty, fought him not only with superb gallantry but with skilful manoeuvre, and wrenched from him the supremacy of the sea.

And meanwhile the army ashore had done the deed whereof the Nemesis has never ceased to pursue it. So far, except for a few intervals too brief to be worth noting, the Commonwealth had been occupied with the business of war, and the principal function of the Parliament had been to provide ways and means for the conduct of war. Incapable of dissolution save by its own act, the House of Commons had resolved just before the execution of the king that it would put an end to itself in three months; but this had been rendered impossible by the Irish and Scotch campaigns.

After the victory of Worcester Cromwell as a private member again brought forward the question of dissolution, but the Rump, as the small remnant that remained after several purgings was called, now showed no disposition to part with the authority which it had so long enjoyed. Frequent conferences were held between the officers of the army and the members of the House, with the only result that the latter introduced a bill which, while providing in some fashion or another for the settlement of the nation, reserved to themselves a perpetuity of power. The army did not conceal its objections to this

---

1. The men were drawn from three Dunbar regiments: Cromwell's own, Goff's and Ingoldsby's, not, alas! from Monk's.

bill; and the climax came when certain members tried to smuggle it through the House before the officers could interfere. Then, April 20th, Cromwell went down to Westminster, and with twenty or thirty musketeers quickly settled the whole matter.

It is difficult to see how things could have ended otherwise. The House had been sufficiently warned at the close of the first civil war that the army would not submit to do all the hard work in order that a handful of civilians might reap the profits. The prestige of that Parliament rested and still rests on the achievements of its armed forces, and it depended for its life on the exertions of men who had subjected themselves for its sake to the restraint of military discipline and to the hardships and dangers of war. The Parliament itself had shown no such devotion and self-sacrifice. While soldiers were in distress for want of the wages due to them, corrupt members were making money; while soldiers were flogged and horsed for drunkenness or fornication, drunkards and lewd livers passed unpunished in the House. Even in matters of administration, if we judge by financial management, the Parliament had not shown extraordinary capacity.

Its difficulties were certainly enormous, but not a few of them had been evaded rather than honestly met. The army, on the other hand, for once contained more than its share of the brains of the nation, and comprehended not less administrative talent and far more patriotic feeling than was to be found in the Parliament. It was therefore too much to expect that it would resign all share in the settlement of the nation to such a body as the Rump. If the question of legality be raised, a House of Commons indissoluble without its own consent, and working without the checks of lords and sovereign, was as unknown to the Constitution as a standing army, and at least as dangerous a menace to liberty. If the Long Parliament taught a salutary lesson to kings, the army taught a lesson no less salutary to parliaments. It would have been better perhaps for the future of the British Army had Cromwell suffered the Rump to remain in power until it should be dissolved in anarchy and confusion, instead of taking the initiative and keeping stern order during the next five dangerous years. But it would have been incomparably worse for England.

Nine months later, after the Little Parliament had been summoned and had in despair resigned its powers, the soldier who had ousted the Rump and taken over its authority to himself was installed, (Dec. 16), as Lord Protector of the Commonwealth of England, Scotland, and Ireland. Since 1652 he had been commander-in-chief, the first in our history, of the forces in all three islands; in virtue of that command he now took over the general government. As was to be expected, he chose his deputies and chief advisers from the officers of the army; and if thereby he placed the realm under military rule we must not allow ourselves to be scared by the phrase from recognition of the worthiness of the administration. There is nothing to make a soldier blush, unless with pride, in the military government of the Protectorate.

Let us begin first with Scotland, which at the close of the Dutch War had been placed under the charge of George Monk. The country was as yet by no means quiet. Agents of Charles Stuart were busy making mischief in the Highlands: and the English found themselves confronted for the first time with the difficulties of a mountain campaign. Monk's predecessor, Robert Lilburn, had essayed the task with but sorry results; Monk himself accomplished it with a success that suffices of itself to stamp him as a great soldier.

Without going into elaborate detail it is worth while to notice his plan for reducing the Highlands. The Royalist forces and their Highland allies were gathered together principally in two districts, in Lochaber under Glencairn, and in Sutherland under Middleton. Monk's design was to cut the Highlands in twain along the line of the present Caledonian Canal, that he might pen his enemy at his will into either half of the country thus divided, and deal with his forces in detail. North of this line the country was sufficiently circumscribed by nature; south of it he was compelled to fix his own boundaries.

The east and south was already guarded by a strong chain of posts running from Inverness through Stirling to Ayr, while one corner to the southwest was secured by the neutrality of the Campbells, which had been gained by diplomacy. Monk now established three independent bases of operations, one at Kilsyth to southward, two more at Perth and Inverness. He then left one column at Dingwall, under Colonel Thomas Morgan, an officer of whom we shall hear more, to hinder the junction of Middleton and Glencairn; and arranged that another column, under Colonel Richard Brayne, of whom also we shall hear more, should sail with all secrecy from Ireland and seize Inverlochy, which was to be his fourth independent base to westward. This done he advanced himself with a third column into the hills from Kilsyth, attacked and defeated Glencairn, and closed the one gap in the net which he had drawn round the Highlands between Loch Lomond and the Clyde.

Then hearing that Middleton had eluded Morgan and passed into

Lochaber, he suddenly shifted his base to Perth and advanced into the heart of the mountains. In two days he had established an advanced magazine at Loch Tay, where the news reached him that the Northern clans had been summoned to assemble at Loch Ness. He at once gave orders that the enemy should be allowed to pass to the southward, and concerted a combined advance of himself, Brayne, and Morgan from the south-west and east to crush him. Unfortunately Morgan, in his eagerness to close in behind the Highlanders, arrived before them and headed them back again to northward. Monk, however, pursued them even thither, hunting them for a week from glen to glen by extraordinary marches, such as the Highlanders had not looked for from mere Englishmen.

Retiring after this raid to Inverness Monk sent Morgan away by sea to threaten the Royalist headquarters at Caithness. The feint was successful. Middleton, who was again in command in the north, at once came down towards the south. His march was seen and reported from the English station at Blair Athol, and Monk was presently on his track over the Grampians. The chase lay through the Drumouchter Pass, Badenoch, Athol, and Breadalbane, thence westward to the head of Loch Awe and back again into Perthshire and over the mountains to Glen Rannoch; and there, as Monk had arranged, Middleton ran straight into the jaws of Morgan's column and was utterly routed. He fled to Caithness with Morgan hard at his heels; while Monk dispersed the few remaining forces of Glencairn in the hills and destroyed every Highland fastness about Loch Lomond.

By August 1654 the work was done; and the Highlands, if ever they may be said to have been conquered, were conquered by George Monk. The English who now wander in thousands over that rugged and enchanting land should remember that the first of their kind that were ever seen therein were Monk's red-coats. [2]

Such very briefly was the first English mountain campaign, admirably designed and admirably executed. The difficulties of military operations in so wild and mountainous a tract were extraordinarily great, and were increased by constant rain and tempest; yet Monk's movements were amazingly rapid. His column on one occasion covered sixty miles in the twenty-four hours. Still more remarkable is his recognition of the fact that in such a campaign success depends mainly

---

2. The elucidation of this campaign Mr. Julian Corbett's *Monk* (Men of Action Series), an admirable sketch of a remarkable man. Monk's letters may be read in Thurloe.

on the efficiency of advanced parties and outposts. He never moved without a cloud of scouts on front and flanks; he made it a rule never to march after mid-day; and when he halted he marked out the camp, and posted every picquet and every sentry himself. He showed himself to be the first English exponent of the principle of savage warfare. He invaded the enemy's country, carrying his supplies with him, and sat down.

If he was attacked he was ready in a strong position; if not, he made good the step that he had taken, left a magazine in a strong post behind him, and marched on, systematically ravaging the country and destroying the newly-sown crops. The enemy was obliged to move or starve, and wherever they went he swiftly followed. If they turned and fought, he asked for nothing better than the chance of dispersing them at a blow; if they dodged, he brought forward another column from another base to cut them off, while he destroyed the fastnesses which they had deserted. Finally, when his work was done he set-tled down quietly to govern the country in a conciliatory spirit. He was able gradually to reduce his military establishment, and, ruling at once with mildness, firmness, watchfulness, and unflagging industry, showed himself to be not less able as an administrator than as a general. Scotland has known many worse rulers and few better than her first English military governor.

In Ireland, after Cromwell's departure, the reduction of the country to order was carried on also by a number of flying columns. Of their leaders but two of the most successful need be named, namely Robert Venables and John Reynolds, the latter Cromwell's kinsman by marriage and sometime captain in his regiment of horse. Ireton had been appointed Lord Deputy on Cromwell's departure, but dying in November 1651 was succeeded by another soldier, Charles Fleet-wood. Though a valuable man when under the command of a strong officer Fleetwood was soon found to be useless when invested with supreme control, and he was soon practically superseded, (1655), by Henry Cromwell, the Protector's second surviving son.

Henry had entered the army at sixteen, had fought with his father in Ireland, and had become a colonel at two-and-twenty. He was ap-pointed, (1657), Lord Deputy of Ireland at the age of twenty-eight. The country was quiet enough at his accession so far as concerned open rebellion; the Tories had been mercilessly hunted down from bog to bog, and the Irish fighting men had been transported in thou-sands by recruiting officers to the armies of Spain and of France. What gallant service they did under Louis the Fourteenth, for they did not greatly love the service of Spain, has been told with just pride by Irish writers; and we too shall encounter some of their regiments before long.

Henry Cromwell's difficulties lay not with the native Irish but with his own officers, the veterans of the Civil War, who were alike jealous of his appointment and insubordinately minded towards the Protector. Immediately on Henry's arrival some of these malcontents held a meeting, wherein they put it to the question whether the present government were or were not according to the Word of God, and carried it in the negative. The very members of the Irish Council, old field-officers who should have known better, were disloyal to him, but being old comrades of Oliver's could not be dismissed. Young as he was, however, Henry gave them clearly to understand that he intended to be master, and therewith proceeded to the difficult, nay impossible, task of executing what is known as the Cromwellian settlement of Ireland. He showed conspicuous ability in extremely trying circumstances, abundant firmness and foresight, and a tolerance of spirit towards the men of other creeds, even Catholics, which was as rare as it was politic. The military governor of Ireland under the Commonwealth was assuredly not a man of whom the British Army need feel ashamed. [3]

Lastly we come to England, where Oliver Cromwell himself sat at the head of the Provisional Government which he was honestly and unceasingly striving to settle on a permanent basis. He defined his own position accurately enough: he was a good constable set to preserve the peace of the parish. But that parish was in a terribly disturbed condition. All that the most visionary could have dreamed of in the subversion of the old order had been accomplished, had even been crowned by the execution of the king; yet still the expected millennium was not yet come. All factions of political and religious dissent, all descriptions of dreamers, of fanatics, of quacks, and of self-seekers had been welded together for the moment by the pressure of the struggle against Royalism and against the rule of alien races. That pressure removed, the whole mass fell asunder into incoherent atoms of sedition and discontent, for which Royalism, as the one element which strove for definite and attainable ends, formed a general rallying-point.

---

3. The best contemporary account of Henry Cromwell's administration will be found in his own letters in Thurloe's *State Papers*.

Good and gallant soldiers who had followed Cromwell on many a field—Harrison, Okey, Overton—fell away into disloyalty. Sexby, who had brought the news of Preston to Westminster, became the most dangerous of conspirators. There is nothing more pathetic in history than the desertions from Cromwell after the establishment of the Protectorate. Nevertheless the misfortune was inevitable, for an army which meddles with politics cannot hope to escape the diseases of politics. Yet, through all this, Cromwell on one point was resolute; he would not allow successful rebellion to be followed by a riot in anarchy. Come what might, he would not suffer indiscipline.

To preserve the peace, however, in such a hot-bed of plots and conspiracies was no easy matter; and before he had been eighteen months Protector, Cromwell brought military government closer home to the people by parcelling England into at first ten and then twelve military districts, each under the command of a major-general. The force at the disposal of these officers for the suppression of disorder varied in the different districts from one hundred to fifteen hundred men, and was composed almost exclusively of cavalry. It amounted on the whole to some six thousand men, all drawn from the militia, who received pay to the amount of eighty thousand pounds annually. Strictly speaking, therefore, it was rather a force of mounted constabulary than of regular cavalry, and there can be no doubt that, if order was to be preserved, such a body of police was absolutely necessary.

Yet it is probable that no measure brought such hatred on the army as this. The magnates of the counties were of course furious at this usurpation of their powers, and the poorer classes resented the intrusion of a soldier and a stranger between themselves and their old masters. After little more than a year the major-generals were abolished, to the general relief and satisfaction. Their brief reign has been forgotten by the army, which can hardly believe that it once took complete charge of the three kingdoms and administered the government on the whole with remarkable efficiency. But the major-generals have not been forgotten by the country. The memory of their dictatorship burned itself deep into the heart of the nation, and even now after two centuries and a half the vengeance of the nation upon the soldier remains insatiate and insatiable.

CHAPTER 8

The Protectorates Foreign Wars

It is now time to pass to the foreign wars of the Protectorate; for though they be little remembered they fairly launched the army on its long career of tropical conquest, and of victory on the continent of Europe.

It is not easy to explain the motives that prompted Cromwell to make an enemy of Spain. He was eagerly courted by both French and Spaniards, and it was open to him to choose whichever he pleased for his allies. The probability is that he was still swayed by the old religious hatred of the days of Elizabeth, and, like her, looked to fill his empty treasury with the spoils of the Indies. He did not perceive that the religious wars of Europe were virtually ended, and that nations were tending already to their old friendships and antagonisms as they existed before the Reformation. Be that as it may, he was hardly firm in the saddle as Protector when he began to frame a great design against the Spanish possessions in the New World. His chief advisers were one Colonel Thomas Modyford of Barbados, who had his own reasons for wishing to ingratiate himself with the Protector, and Thomas Gage, a renegade priest, who had lived long in the Antilles and on the Spanish Main and had written a book on the subject.

The most fitting base of operations was obviously Barbados, which, from its position to windward of the whole Caribbean Archipelago, possessed a strategic importance which it has only lost since the introduction of steam-vessels. It lay ready to Cromwell's hand, having been an English possession since 1628, and was, if Modyford were to be believed, ready to give active assistance in the enterprise. There remained the question whether the expedition should be directed against an island or against the Main. Gage was for the latter course, and named the Orinoco as the objective: Modyford recommended

Cuba or Hispaniola, [1] and Modyford's opinion prevailed.

Gradually the design matured itself, and presently assumed gigantic proportions. A footing once established on one of the Spanish islands to leeward, there was to be a general contest with the Spaniards for the whole of the South Atlantic. Two fleets were to be employed, one in seconding the army's operations on the islands and making raids upon the Main, the other in cruising off the Spanish coast so as to interrupt both plate-fleets from the west and reinforcements from the east. Lastly, not England only, but New England was to play a part in the great campaign. Supplies would be one principal difficulty, but these could be furnished from English America, and not only supplies but settlers, who, trained to self-defence by Indian warfare, should be capable of holding the territory wrested from Spain. Thus the English from both sides of the Atlantic were to close in upon the Spanish dominions in the New World, and turn Nova Hispania into Nova Britannia. There was no lack of breadth and boldness in the design.

All through the latter half of 1654 mysterious preparations went forward with great activity in the English dockyards, and France, Spain, and Holland each trembled lest they might be turned against herself. But the existing organisation in England was unequal to the effort. To equip two fleets of forty and of twenty-five ships for a long and distant cruise was a heavy task in itself; but to add to this the transport of six thousand men over three thousand miles of ocean for an expedition to the tropics was to tax the resources of the naval and military departments to excess.

The burden of the duty fell upon John Desborough, major-general and commissioner of the Admiralty, who was not equal to thinking out the details of such an enterprise nor disposed to give himself much trouble about them. His difficulties were increased by the rascality of contractors, and by the composition of the expeditionary force. By a gigantic error, which has not yet been unlearned, Cromwell, instead of sending complete regiments under their own officers, made up new corps, partly of drafts selected by various colonels and probably containing the men of whom they were most anxious to be rid, and partly of recruits drawn from the most restless and worthless of the nation. He returned in fact to the old system that had so often been found wanting in the days of Elizabeth, of James, and of Charles.

The distribution of command was also faulty. The military commander-in-chief was Robert Venables, who had made a reputation as

---

1. St. Domingo.

a hunter of Tories in Ireland; the admiral joined with him was William Penn, who is unjustly remembered rather as the father of a not wholly admirable Quaker than as one of the ablest and bravest naval officers of his day. But as if two commanders were not already sufficient, there were joined with them three civil commissioners, one Gregory Butler, an officer who had served in the Civil War, Edward Winslow, a civilian and an official, and the Governor of Barbados, Daniel Searle.

There was of course nothing new in the presence of civil commissioners on the staff, and a general's instructions since the days of Henry the Eighth had usually bound him to act by the advice of his Council of War only; but it is abundantly evident that Winslow was employed not only as a commissioner, but as a spy on his colleagues, or on some one of them whose loyalty was suspected. It is strange that so sensible a man as Cromwell should have made such a mistake as this. Monk was the man whom he had wished to send, could he have spared him from Scotland; but failing Monk, Penn and Venables were both of them men who had shown ability in their previous service.

With immense difficulty the expedition was got to sea at the end of December 1654, just two months too late. Even so it sailed without a portion of its stores, which Desborough promised faithfully to send after it without delay. The fleet reached Barbados after a good passage on the 29th of January 1655; and then the troubles began. From too blind faith in the promises of Thomas Modyford, the Protector had trusted to Barbados in great part to equip his army, and to help it on its way. Barbados, from its governor downwards, refused to move a finger. It had no desire to denude itself of arms or of men, and so far from assisting the English threw every possible obstruction in their way.

The planter upon whom Venables had been instructed chiefly to depend was found to be entirely under the thumb of his wife. She was averse to the expedition; and the commissioners, observing her, as they said, to be very powerful and young, abandoned all hope of cooperation from that quarter. Every day too brought fresh evidence of the rotten composition of the force at large, which was without order, without coherency, and without discipline. Unfortunately Venables was not the man to set such failings right. He showed indeed some spasmodic energy, called the Barbadian planters a company of geese, improvised rude pikes of branches of the cabbage-palm, organised a regiment of negroes and a naval brigade, and after several weeks' stay sailed at last for St. Domingo. On the way he picked up a regiment of colonial volunteers which had been collected by Gregory Butler at St. Kitts, and on the 13th of April the expedition was in sight of St. Domingo.

The naval officers were for running in at once and taking the town by a sudden attack. Winslow, the civilian, objected: the soldiers, he said, would plunder the town, and he wanted all spoil for the English treasury. This order against plunder raised something like a mutiny among the troops; but eventually a new plan was chosen, which was probably based on the precedent of Drake in 1586. Venables with three thousand five hundred men sailed to a landing-place thirty miles west of the town, and there disembarked; leaving fifteen hundred more men under a Colonel Buller to land to the eastward of it and march on it from that side. Buller, however, finding it impracticable to obey his instructions, after two days' delay also landed to the westward of the town, though but ten miles from it, at a point called Drake's landing. Elated by a trifling success against a handful of Spaniards who had opposed his disembarkation, he laid aside all thought of co-operation with Venables and pushed on hastily into the jungle to take St. Domingo by himself.

No sooner was he gone, past call or view, when up came Venables to the identical spot where Buller had landed. He had for two days pursued a terrible march of thirty miles through jungle-paths, in the sultry steam of the tropical forest. The men's water-bottles had been left behind in England, and they were choked with thirst; they had torn the fruit from the trees as they passed and had dropped down by scores with dysentery. Hundreds had fallen out, sick and dead, and the column was not only weakened but demoralised.

Next day Venables effected a junction with Buller, and the force, though heartless and spiritless, made shift to creep up to a detached fort which covered the approach to the town. On the way it fell into an ambuscade, and though it beat off the enemy, it lost in the action the only guide who knew where water was to be found, and was compelled to retire ten miles to Drake's landing. There it remained for a week, eating bad food from some scoundrelly contractor's stores, drinking water that was poisoned by a copper mine, and soaked night after night by pouring tropical rain. Dysentery raged with fearful violence, and Venables himself did not escape the plague. Unfortunately, instead of sharing the hardship with his men in camp, he went on board ship to be nursed by Mrs. Venables, who had accompanied him on the voyage. Thus arose open murmurs and scandalous tales, which cost him the confidence of the army.

Nevertheless after six days' rest he again advanced by the same line to the fort from which he had been forced to retreat. To prevent repetition of mishaps from ambuscades he gave strict orders that the advanced guard should throw out flanking parties on each side of the jungle-path. The injunction was disobeyed. The advanced guard walked straight into an ambuscade, two officers fell dead, the third, Adjutant-General Jackson, who was in command, turned and ran; the advanced guard fled headlong back on to the support; the support tumbled back on to the main body, and there, wedged tight in the narrow pass, the English were mown down like grass by the guns of the fort and the lances of the Spanish cavalry.

At last an old colonel contrived to rally a few men in the rear, and advancing with them through the jungle fell upon the flank of the Spaniards and beat them back. He paid for his bravery with his life, but he assured the retreat of the rest of the force, which crept back beaten and crest-fallen to the ships, leaving several colours and three hundred dead men behind it.

Venables and his men were now thoroughly cowed by failure and disease. Penn in vain offered to take the town with his sailors, but Venables and Winslow would not hear of it. All ranks in the fleet now abused the army for rogues, and the worst feeling grew up between the two services. Finally, on the 7th of May, the expedition sailed away in shame to Jamaica. Arrived there, Penn, openly saying that he would not trust the army, led the way himself at the head of the boats of the fleet; and after a trifling resistance the Island was surrendered by capitulation. Then fleet and army began to fight in earnest, officers as well as men; and at last, after the commissioners in command had spent six weeks in incessant quarrelling, Venables and Penn sailed home, leaving the troops and a part of the squadron behind them.

Cromwell's disappointment and chagrin over the failure of his great enterprise were extreme. Both the returned commanders were forthwith sent to the Tower, and though presently released, remained throughout the whole of the Protectorate in disgrace. Still Jamaica had been won and must be held. The command after Venables' departure had devolved on Richard Fortescue, a colonel of the New Model, who, without concealing his infinite contempt for those who had gone home, set himself cheerfully to turn the new possession to account. To him Cromwell wrote letters of encouragement and thanks, with promise of speedy reinforcement. But now a new enemy appeared in Jamaica, one that has laid low many tens of thousands of red-coats, the yellow fever.

In October 1655 the first reinforcements arrived, under command of Major Sedgwicke. He had hardly set foot on the island before Fortescue succumbed, and he could only report that the army was sadly thinned and that hardly a man of the survivors was fit for duty. Then the recruits began to fall down fast, and in a few days the men were dying at the rate of twenty a day. Sedgwicke was completely unnerved; he gave himself up for lost, and in nine months followed Fortescue to the grave. Fresh reinforcements, including all the vaga-bondage of Scotland, were hurried across the Atlantic to meet the same fate. Colonel Brayne, who had served with Monk in Scotland, arrived to succeed Sedgwicke in December 1656.

He lasted ten months, surviving even so two thirds of the men that he brought with him, and then went the way of Sedgwicke and Fortescue. Finally a Colonel D'Oyley, who had sailed with the origi-nal expedition, took over the command, and being a healthy, energetic man, soon reduced things to such order that when in May 1658 the Spaniards attempted to recapture the island, he met and repulsed them with brilliant success. Thus at length was firmly established the Eng-lish possession of Jamaica.

So ended the first great military expedition of the English to the tropics, the first of many attempts, nearly all of them disastrous, to wrest from Spain her Empire in the West. I have dwelt upon it at some length, for it is the opening chapter of a long and melancholy story, whereof one recitation will almost serve for the whole. We have still to go with Wentworth to Carthagena and with Albemarle to Havanna; we shall accompany Abercromby and Moore to St. Vincent and St. Lucia, and other less noted officers to Demarara and Surinam; we shall even see Wellington himself drawing up a plan for operations on the Orinoco: but in spite of a hundred experiences and a thousand warn-ings we shall find the mistakes of Oliver Cromwell eternally repeated, and though we may never again have to tell so disgraceful a story as that of the repulse from St. Domingo, yet we shall seldom fail to en-counter such mournful complaints as were made by Fortescue, Sedg-wicke, and Brayne, of regiments decimated as soon as disembarked, and annihilated before the firing of a shot.

We have now well-nigh learned how to conduct a tropical expe-dition, and life in the tropics is a thing familiar to tens of thousands of Englishmen; but it is worth while to give a thought to these poor soldiers of the Commonwealth. They were the first Englishmen who went to the tropics, not like Drake's crews as fellow-adventurers, but simply as hired fighting men. Yet the traditions of Drake's golden voyages were strong upon them, and they landed, big with expectations of endless gold told up in bags. [4] We can picture their joy at coming ashore, bronzed healthy Englishmen, and their open-mouthed wonder at all that they saw; and then after a few hours the first cases of sickness, the puzzled surgeons with busy lancets, the first death and the first grave; the instant spread of fever on the turning of the virgin soil, and then a hideous iteration of ghastly symptoms, and, sundown after sundown, the row of silent forms and shrouded faces. Englishmen had faced such terrors in the flooded leaguers of Flanders, but it was hard to find them in a fruitful and pleasant land, where the sun shone and the forest grew greener than in England, the loved England that lay so far away over the glorious mocking blue of the tropic sea. [5]

4. Fortescue's own expression. See his letters in Thurloe.
5. The story of the West Indian expedition is very fully told in Thurloe's *State Papers*. There are a few supplementary papers in *Cal. S. P., Col.*, and two accounts in Ogilvy's *History of America* and in the *Harleian Miscellany*.

CHAPTER 9

Flanders

The aggressive attack on St. Domingo at once decided the hostility of Spain towards the Commonwealth, and drove her to take Cromwell's most formidable enemy, Charles Stuart, to her heart. The Protector, on his side, hastened to make treaty of peace and friendship with France which he presently expanded into an offensive and defensive alliance. Mazarin, who had to encounter not only Spain but Condé, was only too glad to welcome the English to his side. By the terms of the treaty it was agreed that the French should provide twenty thousand men, and the English six thousand men, as well as a fleet, for the coming campaign against the Spaniards in Flanders.

Of the English six thousand half were to be paid by France, but the whole were to be commanded by English officers, and reckoned to be the Lord Protector's forces. The plan of campaign was the reduction of the three coast-towns of Mardyck, Dunkirk, and Gravelines, of which the two first were to be made over to England and the third retained by France. Cromwell's great object was to secure a naval station from which he could check any attempted invasion of England by Charles Stuart from Spanish Flanders, and he was therefore urgent that Dunkirk should be first attacked.

Turenne disliked this design, and even threatened to throw up his command if it should be insisted on. To beleaguer Dunkirk without first securing Nieuport, Furnes, and Bergues would, he said, be to be besieged while conducting a siege. But Cromwell had made up his mind that the thing should be done, and, as shall soon be seen, it was done.

Throughout the spring of 1657 therefore preparations for the expedition kept both military and naval departments busily employed, for the fleet was not only to supply the army but to second its operations. The six thousand men, though for the most part old soldiers, were made up of drafts and of new recruits, and were distributed into six regiments. Turenne would gladly have preferred complete corps from the standing Army, but in the existing menace of invasion Cromwell was indisposed to spare them. Nevertheless the new regiments were in perfect order and discipline when they embarked on the 1st of May from Dover for Boulogne. The general in command was Sir John Reynolds, whom we saw lately in Ireland; the major-general was Thomas Morgan, Monk's right-hand man in the Highland war, an impetuous little dragoon known by the name of the "little colonel," [1] and justly reputed to be one of the best officers in the British Isles.

The arrival of the six thousand English foot, all dressed in new redcoats, created a great sensation in France. They were cried up for the best men that ever were seen in the French service; they took precedence of the whole French army, even of the famous Picardie, excepting the Swiss and Scottish body-guards; and they were welcomed by emissaries from the king and Mazarin and inspected by the royal family. It is significant of the difference between the French and English even in their civil wars that the six thousand were amazed to see all the villagers fly from their houses at their approach. They were told that the French soldiery were dreaded as much by their countrymen as by their enemies; and yet Reynolds admitted that the discipline of the French troops was good, for France. "But we," he added proudly, "can lie in a town four days without a single complaint." One thing alone went amiss with the English: they quarrelled with the French ammunition-bread, and clamoured loudly for beef and beer.

By the ill-faith of Mazarin, Reynolds' force instead of marching to Dunkirk was moved inland, and found itself engaged at the siege of St. Venant. Here it gave the Spaniards a taste of its quality. It seems that the English, who were never very happy in handling the spade, were working in some confusion at the advanced trenches when Count Schomberg, a man whom readers should bear in mind, and a few more foreign officers came up and began to pass criticisms. Morgan, wincing under their remarks, impatiently called for a party of fifty men to come to him; whereupon every English soldier in the trenches, incontinently jumped up and without further ado assaulted the town, captured three redoubts, and forced the Spaniards to capitulate. Such blundering gallantry had distinguished the nation since Cocherel, and

---

1. See the pamphlet, *The Bloudie Field*, in King's Pamphlets, British Museum.

was to be repeated on a grander scale at Minden.

But Cromwell was not the man to allow his regiments to be wasted in such operations as these. Dismissing all of Mazarin's excuses as "parcels of words for children," he insisted that the true business of the campaign should be taken in hand at once. In September, therefore, Turenne moved slowly up to the coast; and Cromwell to give him encouragement sent him a reinforcement of two thousand men. Mardyck was easily taken on the 29th of September; but there Turenne stopped. Lockhart, the English ambassador, in vain offered him five of the old regiments of the standing Army if he would proceed at once to the siege of Dunkirk;[2] the great general would not move; and with the capture of Mardyck the campaign of 1657 came to an end.

The English undertook to garrison Mardyck and the town of Bourbourg close to it, and while engaged in this duty incurred the strong censure of Turenne. They kept, he complained, very bad guards, and seemed unable to stand the work of watching; and the failing, it seems, was no new one, for Monk expressed no surprise at hearing of it.

Nevertheless, when on one night in October the Spaniards attempted to surprise Mardyck with five thousand men, they found this unwatchful garrison formidable enough and were repulsed with heavy loss. The truth was that the condition of things in the town was what would now be thought appalling. The winter was unusually severe and the troops very imperfectly protected against it.

Pestilence had broken out among them and men were dying at the rate of ten or twelve a day: once indeed the death-roll within twenty-four hours ran as high as fifty. Reynolds protested in vain, and at last in December he sailed for England to represent matters in person to the Protector. He was cast away on the Goodwin Sands and never seen again. By the time when the season opened for active operations the English had lost since their disembarkation their general and not far from five thousand men.

Lockhart, who took over the command after Reynolds' death in 1658, found the remnant of the army in a very bad state. Discipline was decidedly lax; and the French complained bitterly of the insolence of their allies. This of course was no new thing. So far back as 1603, in the wars of Dutch Independence, a dispute about some firewood had set an English and a French regiment fighting; and the quarrel had ended in the flight of the French to their ships, leaving their colonel

2. Thurloe, vol. vi.

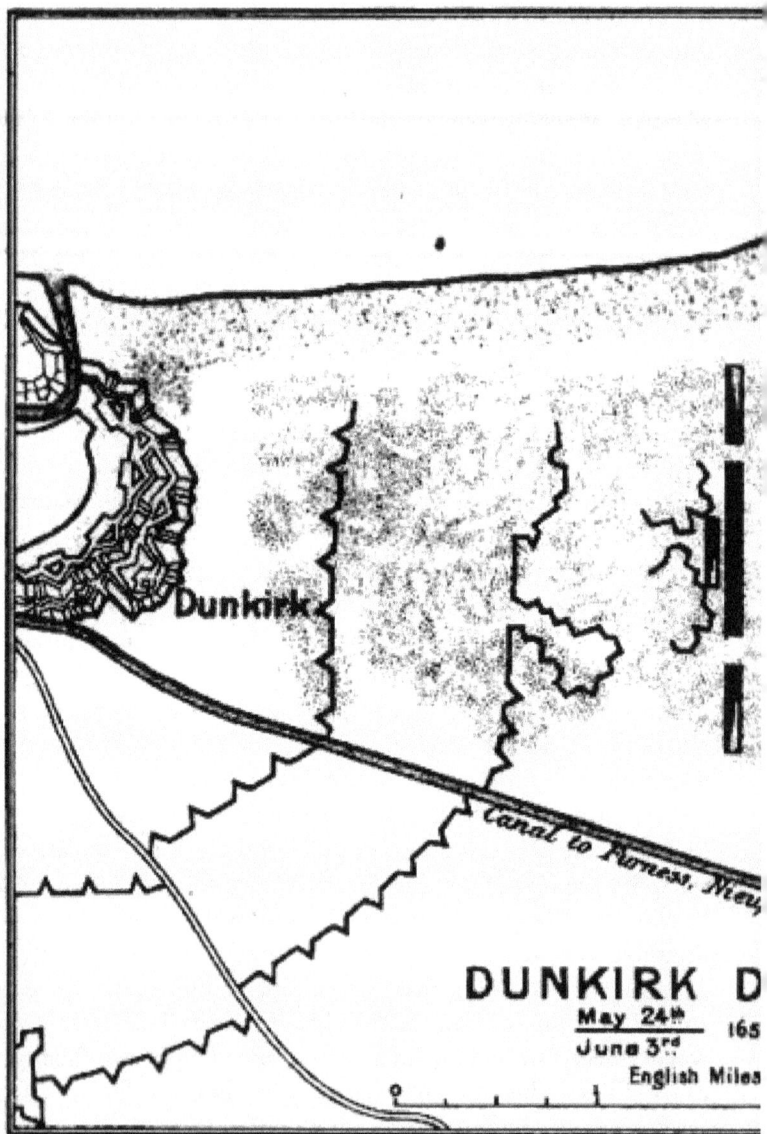

Dunkirk

Canal to Furness, Nieu

DUNKIRK D

May 24th
——————— 165
June 3rd

English Miles

0

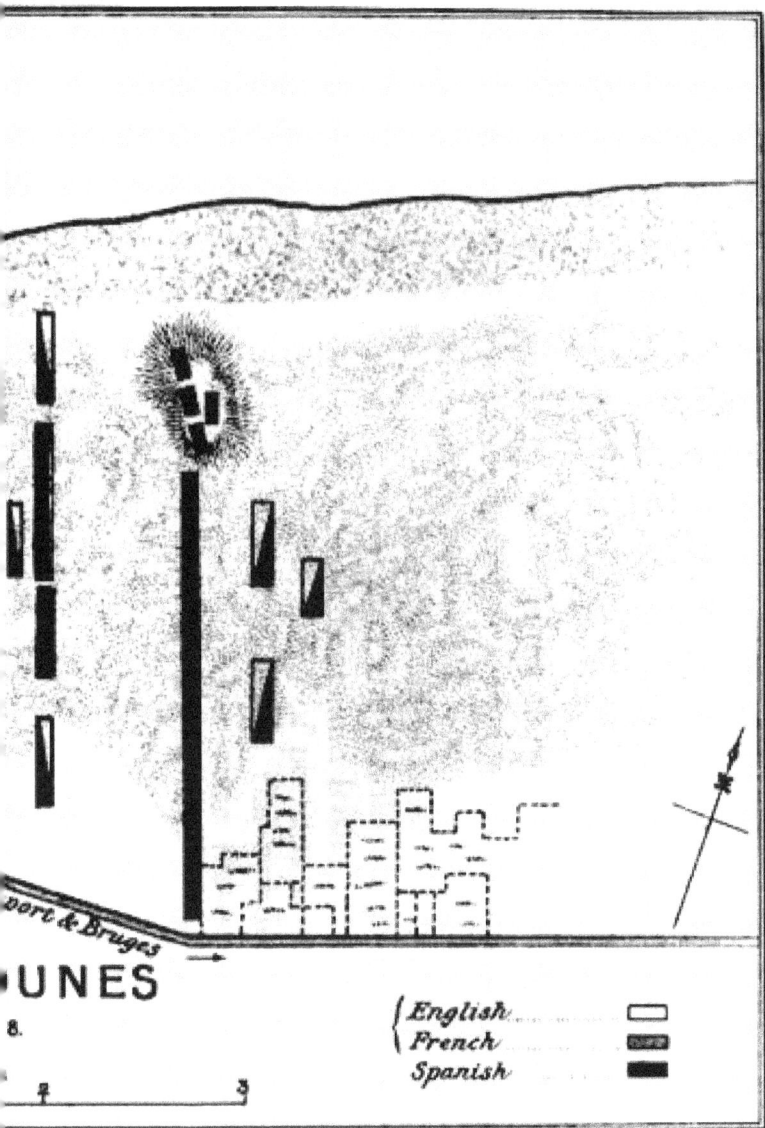

port & Bruges

UNES

8.

	English	□
	French	▨
	Spanish	■

2   3

and sixteen of their comrades dead behind them. [3] The English now, probably on some equally trivial occasion, fell at variance with the French guards and killed several of them; nor could all the frenzy of French indignation avail to obtain the least redress.

Lockhart attributed this insubordinate spirit to the dearth of chaplains; but the true explanation was that over eighty of the officers, disliking the tedium of winter-quarters, had absented themselves, as was customary, from their regiments. When they returned, and four thousand fresh troops with them, Morgan seems to have had little difficulty in restoring discipline.

Morgan opened the campaign before the arrival of March. Lockhart by the capture of two small redoubts that lay on the road to Dunkirk; but it was not till the 4th of May that Turenne broke up his quarters at Amiens, and after a very difficult march to Dunkirk, on the 27th invested the town. A brilliant repulse of a Spanish sortie by the English put him in good humour with his allies, and he was fain to confess that they had done right well. [4] He was to appreciate them still higher within a week; for on the 2nd of June the Spanish Army, fifteen thousand strong, under Don John of Austria, Condé, the Marquis Caracena, and James, Duke of York, drew down to within a mile of his headquarters, with the evident design of forcing the besiegers' lines.

We must pause for a moment over the composition of the motley Spanish host, for there is a part of it under James, Duke of York, with which we are nearly concerned. Five regiments in all, amounting to some two thousand men, were entrusted to the duke's command. Three of these, James's own, Lord Ormonde's, and Lord Bristol's, were Irish, the relics of the loyal party that had been scattered by Cromwell; one, Middleton's, was Scotch, and represented fragments of the force that had been broken up by Monk; and one, which readers must not omit to mark, was English, made up of refugees mostly of gentle birth. It comprehended the last shreds of old English royalism, and was called the King's Regiment of Guards.

Nor must we omit to throw a passing glance at the army of Turenne.

First and foremost there were the six regiments sent out by Cromwell. Then there was a regiment with which we fought at the Battle of Verneuil, 17th August, 1424, the Scottish body-guard of the kings of France. Next, there was a regiment which passed from the

---

3. Collins, *State Papers* (July 1603).

4. "*Les Anglais y firent fort bien.*" See his letter in Thurloe.

Swedish to the French service in 1635, Regiment Douglas, some time the Scots Brigade of King Gustavus Adolphus. It had passed through many campaigns and absorbed other corps of British within the past twenty years, and could now add the names of Rocroi, Lens and Fribourg to its records; but here it was, newly recruited from Scotland by the Protector's permission, marching side by side with the red-coats, though quite unconscious how soon it was destined to take its place among them, to fight the Battle of Dunkirk Dunes. Lastly, an Irish regiment, known by the name of Dillon, and made up of men who had fled from the wrath of Cromwell, completed the strange representation of the united Commonwealth. [5]

It was evening of the 2nd of June before Turenne could satisfy himself that the whole of the Spanish Army was present before him, but no sooner was he assured of it than he resolved to fight on the morrow. The English were still at Mardyck, and the orders reached Lockhart so late and came as such a surprise that the marshal politely intimated his wish to give reasons for his determination. "I take the reasons for granted," answered Lockhart, "it will be time to hear them when the battle is over."

At ten o'clock the English marched off, Lockhart, who was suffering agonies from stone, driving in his carriage at their head, and at daybreak reached Turenne's headquarters. The next three hours were spent in drawing up the line of battle, which was of the mathematical precise type that prevailed in those days. In the first line there were thirteen troops of cavalry on the right wing, as many on the left, and eleven battalions of infantry in the centre; in the second line there were ten troops on the right, nine on the left, and seven battalions in the centre. Five troops of horse were posted midway between the two lines of infantry, and four more were held in reserve. The whole force was reckoned at six thousand horse and nine thousand foot, of which latter the English contingent made more than half. The place assigned to the red-coats was the left centre, which, if not the post of honour, was assuredly the post of danger.

Don John's line of battle was widely different. He had taken up a strong position among the sand hills, facing west, his right resting on the beach, his left on the Bruges Canal; and the whole of his infantry was drawn up in his first line. A sand hill higher than the rest on his right was regarded as the key of the position, and was strongly held,

---

5. It must be remembered that this was no figure of speech. Cromwell was the first who gathered in representatives of Scotland and Ireland to Westminster.

as the place of honour, by four Spanish regiments. Next to them on their left stood the five regiments under the Duke of York, with one battalion in reserve, and the line was continued by battalions of Germans and Walloons. The Spanish horse was massed behind the foot in columns according as the sand hills permitted; and the whole force numbered between fourteen and fifteen thousand men.

Notwithstanding that they had marched all night, and in spite of Turenne's orders that the line should dress by the right, the English outstrode the French in the advance and began the action alone. The position occupied by the Spaniards in their front was so strong, that Lockhart by his own confession despaired of carrying it. Lieutenant-Colonel Fenwick however, who commanded Lockhart's regiment, undertook the task without the general's instructions. Covered by a cloud of skirmishers he advanced steadily with his pikes to the foot of the sand hill, and while the musketeers wheeling right and left maintained a steady fire, he calmly halted the pikes to let the men take breath. Then with a joyful shout they swarmed up the treacherous sand and went straight at the Spaniards. Fenwick fell at once, mortally wounded by a musket shot; his major, Hinton, took his place, and was also shot down.

Officer after officer fell, but the men were not to be checked, and though the Spaniards, backed by a company of the English guards, fought hard and well, they were fairly swept off the sand hill, and retired in confusion, leaving nine out of thirteen captains dead on the ground. James, Duke of York, tried to save the rout by charging Lockhart's victorious regiment with his single troop of horse, but he was beaten back, and though at a second attempt he succeeded in breaking into its flank he met with so sturdy a resistance from every isolated man as convinced him that his effort was hopeless. Meanwhile the rest of the English regiments advanced quickly in support; the French horse on the left wing came up likewise, and the rout of the Spanish right was complete.

With the uncovering of its right flank the whole of Don John's line wavered, and few regiments, except those under the immediate direction of Condé, far away on the left, showed more than a feeble resistance to the advancing French. Very soon the whole force—Spaniards, Walloons and Germans, Scots and Irish—were in full retreat, and a single small corps of perhaps three hundred men stood isolated and alone in the position among the sand hills. A French officer rode forward and summoned the little party to surrender. "We were posted here by the Duke of York," was the answer, "and mean to hold our ground as long as we can."

The Frenchman explained that resistance was hopeless. "We are not accustomed to believe our enemies," was the reply. "Then look for yourself," rejoined the Frenchman; and leading the commander to the top of a sand hill he showed him the retreating army of Spain. Thereupon the solitary regiment laid down its arms: it was the English King's Royal Regiment of Guards. [6]

The losses of the victorious English were very severe. In Lockhart's regiment but six out of the whole number of officers and sergeants had escaped unhurt; and the honours of the day were admitted by all to lie with the red-coats. The action led to the speedy fall of Dunkirk; and Lockhart, being reinforced by two regiments from England, was able to detach four to continue the campaign under the command of Morgan. Bergues, Dixmuyde, and Oudenarde fell in quick succession, and little opposition was encountered until the siege of Ypres, where the English delivered so daring and brilliant an assault that Turenne, overcome with admiration, embraced their leader, Morgan, and called him one of the bravest captains of the time. The capture of Ypres was the last exploit of the six thousand—the immortal six thousand, as they were styled in the admiring pamphlets of the day. After an advance almost to the walls of Brussels, the campaign came to an end; Morgan returned to England to receive knighthood, and the English retired to Dunkirk to spend another winter in cold and misery and want, and worst of all in deep uncertainty for the future. [7]

6, Clarke's *James II*.

7. The best English source for the account of the campaign in Flanders is Thurloe's *State Papers*; there are also some curious details in a tract in the *Harleian Miscellany*, which, however, I have accepted only when confirmed by newspapers. Bussy Rabutin's *Memoires*, and Clarke's *James II*. are among other authorities.

CHAPTER 10

Monk

For even while Morgan was watching the Spanish garrison march out of Ypres, the soldier who had made the English Army was lying speechless and unconscious at St. James's, worn out with many campaigns and with the work of keeping the peace in England. Before tattoo sounded on the 3rd of September 1658, Oliver Cromwell was dead, and no man could say who should come after him. Richard Cromwell, his son, held two trump-cards in his hand—Henry Cromwell and the army in Ireland, George Monk and his army in Scotland.

He was afraid to play either, and yielded up his power, (April 21), to a clique of his father's old officers—Fleetwood, Desborough, and others—who brought back the Rump of the Long Parliament to reign in his stead. Henry Cromwell resigned his command, and the power of the Cromwells was gone. The Rump now took over Cromwell's bodyguard for its own protection, and to make the army thoroughly subservient decided that all officers should be approved by itself, and all commissions signed by the Speaker. So large was the military establishment that this work of revising the list of officers was never completed. George Monk, however, accepted the Speaker's commission without a word.

It was not in the nature of things that the English generals should long submit to the *junto* of politicians which it had set over England. In a very short time the leaders of the army for the second time cleared away the Rump, and took the supreme power into their own hands; but herein they overlooked the existence of the ablest soldier left in Great Britain. Monk was ready enough to take his orders from Oliver Cromwell, but not from such small men as Lambert and Desborough. No sooner did the news of the new departure reach him at Dalkeith,

94

(October 17), than with amazing rapidity he secured every garrison in Scotland, seized the bridge over the Tweed at Berwick, purged his troops of all officers disloyal to the Parliament, and gave orders for his whole force to concentrate at Edinburgh.

Morgan, with the glories of Flanders still fresh on him, presently came to help him in the reorganisation of his army, and by the middle of November he began to move slowly south. Negotiations with the English leaders had been in progress ever since Monk first took decided action, and, though fully aware that they must come to nothing, he was not sorry to gain a little time in order to establish discipline thoroughly in the force under his command. By the end of November he had fixed his headquarters at Berwick.

There, at one o'clock on the morning of the 7th of December, he was surprised by the news that, in spite of much peaceful profession, the English general Lambert had besieged Chillingham Castle and had marched within twenty miles of the Border. One hour sufficed for Monk to write the necessary orders for the movement of the troops, and at two o'clock he was in the saddle and away to inspect the fords of the Tweed. The night was stormy and pitch dark, and the roads were sheets of ice, but on he galloped, despite the entreaties of his staff, through wind and sleet, up hill and down, at dangerous speed. "It was God's infinite mercy that we had not our necks broke," wrote one who was an unwilling partaker of that ride. [1]

By eleven o'clock the inspection was over and headquarters were fixed at Coldstream. A regiment of foot had already arrived there to guard the ford before the general came, and had cleared away every scrap of provisions. His staff-officers dispersed to find food where they could, but George Monk put a quid of tobacco into his cheek and sat down contented with a good morning's work. He had occupied every pass from Berwick to Kelso, and had so thought out every detail that he could concentrate his whole force at any given point in four hours. The bulk of his troops under Morgan were stationed on the exposed flank at Kelso; he himself was in the centre at Coldstream. Lambert might attack his front or turn his flank if he dared.

For three weeks Monk's army lay in this position, four regiments of horse and six of foot, [2] waiting for the moment to advance. The cold was intense, and the quarters in the little village of Coldstream were very strait. The general occupied a hovel wherein he had hardly

---

1. Gumble, the chaplain, from whose *Life of Monk* this account is taken.
2. According to the usual establishment, 9600 men besides officers.

space to turn round, and the men suffered greatly from privation and hard weather, but Monk's spirit kept them all in cheerfulness, and those who had shared his hardships never ceased to boast themselves to be Coldstreamers. At last, on the 31st of December, came the news that the army which had deposed the Rump was up in mutiny; and at daybreak of the 1st of January 1660 Monk's army crossed the Tweed in two brigades and began its memorable march to the south.

All day they tramped knee-deep through the snow, full fifteen miles to Wooler, while the advanced-guard of horse by a marvellous march actually covered the fifty miles to Morpeth. At York they were met by Fairfax, who had roused himself at such a crisis for a last turn of military duty, and picking up deserters on every side from Lambert's regiments they increased their strength at every march. On the 31st of January Monk received at St. Albans the Parliament's confirmation of his commission as general, and three days later he occupied London. His own regiment of foot was quartered for the first time in and about St. James's.

It is unnecessary to dwell on the intricate movements in the political world during the three following months; it must suffice to say that Monk was finally obliged to coerce the Rump as all other soldiers had coerced it. In spite of all engagements to dissolve itself without delay, this pretentious little assembly still clung, notwithstanding its unpopularity, to power; but a letter from the general was sufficient to bring it to reason without a file of musketeers. Such a letter arrived on the 6th of April; and though the House resolved not to read it until it had gratified its vanity by a little further debating, yet it decided after opening it to make the question of dissolution its very next business. Before evening it had ceased to exist. One last desperate attempt of Desborough and Lambert to divide the army was suppressed with Monk's habitual promptitude, and on the 1st of May the general, sitting as member for his native county in a new House of Commons, moved that the king should be invited to England. Three weeks later Monk's life-guard and five regiments of horse escorted the restored monarch, Charles II, into London; and the work of the New Model Army was done.

CHAPTER 11

Discipline of the Army

It is strange that our historians have for the most part taken leave of the New Model without a tinge of regret, without estimation of its merits or enumeration of its services. Mountains of eulogy have been heaped on the Long Parliament, but little has been spared for this famous army; nay, even military historians by a strange perversity begin the history of the Army not from its foundation but from its dissolution. Much doubtless besides the creation of a standing army dates from the great rebellion, though few things more important in our history, unless indeed it be the cant that denies its importance. The bare thought of militarism or the military spirit is supposed to be unendurable to Englishmen. As if a nation had ever risen to great empire that did not possess the military spirit, and as if England herself had not won her vast dominions by the sword. We are accustomed to speak of our rule as an earnest for the eternal furtherance of civilisation; but we try to conceal the fact that the first step to empire is conquest. It is because we are a fighting people that we have risen to greatness, and it is as a fighting people that we stand or fall. Arms rule the world; and war, the supreme test of moral and physical greatness, remains eternally the touchstone of nations.

Surely therefore the revival of the military spirit, and on the whole the grandest manifestation of the same in English history, are not matters to be lightly overlooked. The campaigns of the Plantagenets had shown how deep was the instinct of pugnacity that underlay the stolid English calm, but since the accession of the Tudors no sovereign had given it an outlet ashore in any great national enterprise. Elizabeth never truly threw in her lot with the revolted Netherlands; James hated a soldier, and shrank back in terror from the idea of throwing the English sword into the scale of the Thirty Years' War; Charles's miserable trifling with warfare contributed not a little to the unpopularity which caused his downfall. The English were compelled to sate their military appetite in the service of foreign countries, and as fractions of foreign armies.

Then at last the door of the rebellion was opened and the nation crowded in. It is hardly too much to say that for at any rate the four years from 1642 to 1646 the English went mad about military matters. Military figures and metaphors abounded in the language and literature of the day, and were used by none more effectively than by John Milton. [1] Divines took words of command and the phrases of the parade ground as titles for their discourses, and were not ashamed to publish sermons under such a head as "As you were." If anything like a review or a sham fight were going forward, the people thronged in crowds to witness it; and one astute colonel took advantage of this feeling to reconcile the people to the prohibition of the sports of May-day. He drew out two regiments on Blackheath, and held a sham fight of Cavaliers and Roundheads, wherein both sides played their parts with great spirit and the Cavaliers were duly defeated; and the spectacle, we are assured, satisfied the people as well as if they had gone maying any other way.

It is true that the sentiment did not endure, that the eulogy of the general and his brave soldiers was turned in time to abuse of the tyrant and his red-coats; but when a nation after beheading a king, abolishing a House of Lords, and welcoming freedom by the blessing of God restored, still finds that the golden age is not yet returned, it must needs visit its disappointment upon someone. The later unpopularity of the strong military hand does not affect the undoubted fact of a great preliminary outburst of military enthusiasm. Nor indeed even at the end was there any feeling but of pride in the prowess of Morgan's regiments in Flanders. The rapid advance of military reform in its deepest significance is not less remarkable. For two years it may be said that opposing factions of the Civil War fought at haphazard, after the obsolete fashion of the days of the Tudors. The most brilliant soldier on either side was a military adventurer of the type that Shakespeare had depicted, a man who:

dreams of cutting Spanish throats,
Of trenches, ambuscadoes, Spanish blades
And healths five fathoms deep.

---

1. It is not I think irrelevant in this connection to remind the reader of the military manoeuvres of the rebel angels in *Paradise Lost.*

98

Against the wild, impetuous Rupert the primitive armies of the Parliament were powerless. From the first engagement Cromwell perceived that such high-mettled dare-devils could be beaten only by men who took their profession seriously, who made some conscience of what they did, who drew no distinction between moral and military virtues, who believed that a bad man could not be a good soldier, nor a bad soldier a good man, who saw in cowardice a moral failing and in vice a military crime. Cromwell's system is generally summed up in the word fanaticism; but this is less than half of the truth. The employment of the phrase, moral force, in relation to the operations of war, is familiar enough in our language; but the French term *morale* is now pressed into the service to signify that indefinable consciousness of superiority which is the chief element of strength in an army. Such narrowing of old broad terms is in a high degree misleading.

It should never be forgotten that military discipline rests at bottom on the broadest and deepest of moral foundations; its ideal is the organised abnegation of self. Simple fanaticism is in its nature undisciplined; it is strong because it assumes its superiority, it is weak because it is content with the assumption; only when bound under a yoke such as that of a Zizka or of a Cromwell is it irresistible. Cromwell's great work was the same as Zizka's, to subject the fanaticism that he saw around him to discipline. He did not go out of his way to find fanatics. He once wrote:

Sir, the State in choosing men for its service takes no notice of their opinions; if they be willing faithfully to serve it, that satisfies.

In forming his original regiment of horse he undoubtedly selected men of good character, just as any colonel would endeavour to do today, (1899). But Fairfax's was by no means an army of saints. One regiment of the New Model mutinied when its colonel opened his command with a sermon, and the Parliament with great good sense prohibited by Ordinance the preaching of laymen in the army. It is time to have done with all misconceptions as to the work that Cromwell did for the military service of England, for it is summed up in the one word discipline. It was the work not of a preacher but of a soldier.

That the discipline was immensely strict and the punishments correspondingly severe followed necessarily from the nature of his system. The military code took cognisance not only of purely military offences, but of many moral delinquencies, even in time of peace, which if now visited with the like severity would make the list of defaulters as long as the muster-roll. Swearing was checked principally by fine, drunkenness by the wooden horse. This barbarous engine, imitated from abroad, consisted simply of a triangular block of wood, like a saddle-stand, raised on four legs and finished with a rude representation of a horse's head. On this the culprit was set astride for one hour a day for so many days, with from one to six muskets tied to his heels; and that degradation might be added to the penalty, drunkards rode the horse in some public place, such as Charing Cross, with cans about their necks.

A soldier who brought discredit on his cloth by public misconduct paid the penalty with public disgrace. Fornication was commonly punished with the lash, the culprit being flogged so many times up and down the ranks of his company or regiment according to the flagrancy of the offence. It is small wonder that men forced by such discipline to perpetual self-control should have scorned civilians who allowed themselves greater latitude, and despised a Parliament which, in spite of many purgings, was never wholly purged of loose livers.

Towards the unfortunate Royalists the feelings of the Parliamentary Army after 1645 were of unutterable contempt. It was not only that it felt its moral superiority over the unhappy cavaliers; it mingled with this the keenest professional pride. No sergeant-major of the smartest modern cavalry regiment could speak with more withering disdain of the rudest troop of rustic yeomanry than did the Parliamentary newspapers of the prisoners captured at Bristol. [2] It is instructive, too, to note the patronising tone adopted by Reynolds towards the army of Turenne, his criticism of the discipline that was "good, for France," and his observations as to the proverbial inefficiency of a French regiment at the end of a campaign. Beyond all doubt the English standing army from 1646 to 1658 was the finest force in Europe. It is the more amazing that Cromwell should have suffered its fair fame to be tarnished by the rabble that he sent to the West Indies.

---

2. "First came half-a-dozen of carbines in their leathern coats and starved weather-beaten jades, just like so many brewers in their jerkins made of old boots, riding to fetch in old casks; and after them as many light horsemen with great saddles and old broken pistols, and scarce a sword among them, just like so many fiddlers with their fiddles in cases by their horses' sides. . . . In the works at Bristol was a company of footmen with knapsacks and half pikes, like so many tinkers with budgets at their backs, and some musketeers with *bandoliers* about their necks like a company of sow-gelders."—*Newspaper*. (Reference unfortunately lost.)

Such an army will never again be seen in England; but though its peculiar distinctions are for ever lost, the legacies bequeathed by it must not be overlooked. Enough has been said of the institution of the new discipline, and of the virtual extinction of the old stamp of military adventurer; it remains now briefly to summarise the minor changes wrought by the creation of a standing Army. First comes the incipient organisation of a War-Department as seen in the Committee of the Army working with the Treasurers at War on one side and the ancient Office of Ordnance on the other, and in the appointment of a single commander-in-chief for all the forces in England, Scotland, and Ireland. And here it must be noted in passing that the division of the army into an English, Scotch, and Irish establishment, which lasted until the three kingdoms were one by one united, becomes fully defined in the years of the Protectorate.

Next must be mentioned the organisation of regiments with frames of a fixed strength, regiments of horse with six troops, and of foot and dragoons with ten companies, and the maintenance of a fixed establishment for services of artillery and transport. [3] Further, to combine the unity of the army with the distinction of the various corps that composed it, there was the adoption of the historic scarlet uniform differenced by the facings of the several regiments.

Clothing however, leads us to the more complicated question of the pay of the army. The regular payment of wages was, as has been seen, the first essential step towards the establishment of a standing force; and with it came concurrently the system of clothing, mounting and equipping soldiers at the expense of the State. It should seem, however, that the rules for regulating the system were sufficiently elastic, for we find quite late in the second Civil War that troopers generally still provided their own horses, and received a higher rate of pay, and that colonels were permitted to make independent contracts for the clothing and equipment of their regiments. The stoppages from the soldiers' pay at this period are also instructive. The deduction of a fixed sum for clothing dates, as has been already told, from the days of Elizabeth if not from still earlier times. But to this was now added the principle of withholding a proportion of the wages, under the name of arrears, as security against misconduct and desertion; while it was a recognised rule that both men and officers should forfeit an additional

---

3. This is evident from the mention of the "train" in the list in the *Commons Journals*, September 1651. The field-train was then transferred to Scotland bodily, where we find it still in December 1652 and again in 1659 (April). See *Commons Journals*.

proportion so long as they lived at free quarter.

An allowance for billet-money, and a fixed tariff of prices to be paid by soldiers while on the march within the kingdom, contributed somewhat to lighten the burden of all these stoppages, and made a precedent for the Mutiny Act of a later day. It is worthy of remark that the garrison of Dunkirk found in the town special buildings, constructed by the Spaniards for their troops and called barracks,[4] and that it was duly installed therein in the autumn of 1659. The reader, if he have patience to follow me further, will be able to note for himself how long was the time before English soldiers exchanged life in ale-houses for the Spanish system of life in barracks.

But there is another and more interesting aspect of the question of pay, when we pass from that of the men to that of the officers. The extinction of the old military adventurer brought with it the total abolition, for the time, of the system of purchase. In the Royalist regiments that gathered around Charles Stuart in Flanders, we find that companies and regiments still changed hands for money, but in the English standing Army the practice seems utterly to have disappeared. Promotion was regulated not necessarily by seniority but by the recommendation of superior officers, and, as external evidence seems to indicate, ran not in individual regiments but in the army at large.

The arrears of officers, especially of those who possessed means of their own, often remained, through their patriotic forbearance, not only many months but many years overdue; and it is interesting to mark that their inability to watch over their own interests while they were engaged on active service led to the appointment of regimental agents, who drew their pay and transacted their financial business with the country on their behalf. The Army Agent may, therefore, justly boast himself to be a survival of the Civil War.

Nor can I leave this subject without reference to yet another remarkable feature in the New Model Army, which unfortunately has not passed into a tradition. I allude to the great and sudden check on the ancient evil of military corruption. To say that corruption came absolutely to an end would be an excessive statement, for the minutes of courts-martial on fraudulent auditors are still extant, but it is probable that during the Civil War it was reduced to the lowest level that it has touched in the whole of our army's history. The abolition

---

4. Thurloe, vol. vii. This is the first passage in which I have encountered the word thus spelt: "certain buildings . . . called the barracks or Spanish quarters." But there is mention of a *baraque* in the besiegers' lines before Ostend in 1604. *Grimeston.*

of purchase and the higher moral tone that pervaded the whole force doubtless contributed greatly to so desirable an end. It is, however, melancholy to record that the evil was evidently but scotched, not killed.

Before the Protector had been dead a year, there was seen, at the withdrawal of part of the garrison of Dunkirk, a deliberate and disgraceful falsification of the muster-rolls, aggravated by every circumstance that could encourage fraud and injure good discipline. Contact with foreign troops was probably the immediate cause of this lamentable backsliding, but it furnishes a sad commentary on the fickleness of Puritan morality.

Finally, let us close with the greatest and noblest work of the New Model Army, the establishment of England's supremacy in the British Isles as a first step to their constitutional union. No achievement could have stood in more direct antagonism to the policy of Charles Stuart, who strove with might and main to set nation, against nation and kingdom against kingdom, and paid for his folly with his life.

It may be that the greatness of this service will in these days be denied. There were not wanting in the Long Parliament men who intrigued with Scotland against England rather than suffer power to slip from their hands, and it is not perhaps strange that the type of such men should be imperishable. Those, however, who call England the predominant partner in the British Isles should not forget who were the men that made her predominant. [5] The Civil War was no mere rebellion against despotic authority. It accomplished more than the destruction of the old monarchy; it was the battle for the union of the British Isles, and it was fought and won by the New Model Army.

---

5. It is curious to note that a vote for a statue of Oliver Cromwell was in 1895 moved by the party that proposes to undo his work, and was defeated by the party that wishes to continue it. The supporters of the Union deliberately refused this tardy honour to the man who did more than any other to accomplish the Union, and who actually was the first to summon representatives from Scotland and Ireland to Westminster. Whether either party was sincere may well be considered doubtful.

CHAPTER 12

The Birth of the Modern British Army

The restoration of the Stuarts had been to all outward semblance effected, Charles had been escorted through the streets of London by the horse of the New Model, and yet the power which had practically ruled England since 1647 was still unbroken. The problem which the Long Parliament had treated with such disastrous contempt in that year was still unsolved; and there could be no assurance of stability for the monarchy until the army should be disbanded. As to the manner in which this most difficult task must be accomplished the events of 1647 had given sufficient warning, for an army of sixty-five thousand men was even less to be trifled with than the comparatively small force of the second year of the New Model. Disbandment must not be hurried, and all arrears of pay must be faithfully discharged. Still the work could not but be both delicate and dangerous, requiring good faith and a tact that could only be found in a soldier who understood soldiers and a man who understood men. Fortunately such a man and such a soldier was to hand in the person of George Monk.

His scheme was soon prepared and adopted by Parliament. The regiments were to be broken up gradually, the order of disbandment being determined by lot, with the reservation that Monk's own regiments of horse and foot, together with two others that had been taken over by the Dukes of York and Gloucester, [1] should be kept until the last. An act copied from an Ordinance of the Commonwealth was passed, to enable discharged soldiers to engage in trades without preliminary apprenticeship, and thus to facilitate their return to civil

---

1. The Duke of Gloucester died in the same year.

life. By extraordinary exertions the needful money was raised, and the work proceeded apace. It seemed as if the close of the year 1660, according to the old reckoning which began the new year on the 25th of March, would have seen it completed, for by the first week in January the hand of disbandment had reached Monk's regiment of horse.

There however it was stayed. On the 6th of January an insurrection of fifth-monarchy men, a fanatical sect which had felt the might of Cromwell's repressing arm, not only saved the last relic of the New Model, but laid the foundation stone of a new army. The rising was not suppressed without difficulty, not indeed until the veterans of Monk's regiment of foot, to whom such work was child's play, came up and swept it contemptuously away. The outbreak showed the need of keeping a small permanent force for the security of the king's person. The disbandment of this regiment and of the troop of horse-guards which had been assigned to Monk on his first arrival in London was thereupon countermanded, and the king gave orders for the raising of a new regiment of Guards in twelve companies, to be commanded by Colonel John Russell; of a regiment of horse in eight troops to be commanded by the Earl of Oxford; and of a troop of horse-guards, to be commanded by Lord Gerard. The Duke of York's troop of horse-guards, the same which he had led to an unsuccessful charge at Dunkirk Dunes, was also summoned home from Dunkirk.

The first stones of the new army being thus laid, there remained nothing but formally to abolish, in accordance with the letter of the Act of Parliament, the last remnant of the New Model. On the 14th of February, 1661 Monk's regiment of foot was mustered on Tower Hill, where it solemnly laid down its arms, and as solemnly took them up again, with great rejoicing, as the Lord General's regiment of Foot-Guards. But to England at large this corps had but one name, that which still survives in its present title of the Coldstream Guards. Though ranking second on the list of our infantry, this is the senior regiment of the British Army. Other corps may boast of earlier traditions, but this is the oldest national regiment and the sole survivor of the famous New Model. Well may it claim, in its proud Latin motto, that it is *second to none*.

Colonel Russell's regiment, being the King's Own regiment of Guards, and raised specially for the protection of his person, obtained precedence not unnaturally of its earlier rival, and presently, by absorbing the handful of gallant men who had refused to surrender at Dunkirk Dunes, established its claim to represent the defeated cavaliers, as the Coldstream represent the victorious Roundheads, in the long contest of the Civil War. It is the regiment once called the First Guards, and now the Grenadier Guards, and it has known little of defeat since it ceased to fight against its countrymen.

The two troops of Life-Guards—the first the king's, commanded by Lord Gerard, the second the Duke of York's own—took precedence in like manner of Monk's Life-Guard; and after long existence as independent troops, blossomed at last into the First and Second regiments of Life-Guards that now stand at the head of our army list. They were composed of men of birth and education, and for more than a century were rightly called gentlemen of the Life-Guards. Cromwell too had possessed such a guard, for he knew the value of gentlemen who had courage, honour, and resolution in them. Thus they stood apart from Lord Oxford's regiment of horse, which is still known to us from the colour of its uniform by its original name of the Blues. This corps was almost certainly made up of disbanded troopers of the New Model, of which there was no lack at that time in England; [2] while its colonel brought to it traditions of still earlier days in the honoured name of Vere.

But there was yet another regiment to be gathered in from the battlefield of Dunkirk Dunes, this time not from the defeated but from the victorious army. In view of the peril of the king from Venner's insurrection, Louis the Fourteenth was requested to restore to him the regiment of Douglas, the representative of the Scots Brigade of Gustavus Adolphus; and this famous corps, having duly arrived in the year 1662, became the Royal or Scots regiment, and took the place which it still occupies at the head of the infantry of the Line under the old title of the Royal Scots. It returned to France in 1662 and did not return permanently to the English service until 1670, but it retained its precedence and it retains it still.

So far for the king's provision for his own safety. But it was also necessary for him to provide himself with money, and this he did in the simplest fashion by marrying an heiress, Catherine, Princess of Portugal, who brought him half a million of money, Bombay and Tangier, to say nothing of promises of pecuniary aid from Louis the Fourteenth, who encouraged the match for his own ends. Tangier being in constant peril of recapture by the Moors was a troublesome possession, and required a garrison, for which duty a regiment of foot

---

2. I find no sufficient ground for assuming that the regiment was Unton Crook's of the New Model, which had been disbanded two months before.

and a strong troop of horse were raised by the Earl of Peterborough, the recruits being furnished mainly by the garrison of Dunkirk. These corps also survive among us, (1899), as the Second or Queen's regiment of Foot, and the First or Royal Dragoons.

Concurrently in this same year 1661 an act was passed for the re organisation of the militia. The obligations to provide horse-men and foot-men were distributed, following the venerable precedent of the statute of Winchester, according to a graduated scale of property, and the complete control of each county's force was committed to the lord-lieutenant. To him also were entrusted powers to organise the force into regiments and companies, to appoint officers, and to levy rates for the supply of ammunition. Finally, the supreme command of the militia, over which the Long Parliament had fought so bitterly with Charles the First, was restored to the king, together with that of all forces by sea and land.

CHAPTER 13

The Expansion of Empire

So much was accomplished in the first two years of Charles the Second. It sufficed for two years longer, when English commercial enterprise involved the restored monarchy in its first war. In truth it is hardly recognised how powerfully the spirit of adventure and colonisation had manifested itself under the Stuarts. The Empire indeed was growing fast. In 1661 England already possessed the New England States, Maryland and Virginia, as well as, for the time, Acadia, Nova Scotia, and Newfoundland. Off the American coast the Bermudas were hers; in the Caribbean Archipelago Barbados, Antigua, Montserrat, Nevis, St. Kitts, and Jamaica were settled; while Dominica, St. Lucia, St. Vincent, and Tobago, though not yet wrested from the Caribs, were reckoned subject to the British Crown. In 1663 one Company received a charter for the settlement of Carolina, and another, the Royal African, which enjoyed the monopoly of the trade in negro slaves, had fixed its headquarters at Cape Coast Castle. Nor must it be omitted that the East India Company, originally incorporated in 1599, received in 1660 a second charter conferring ampler powers, most notably in respect of military matters.

England, however, had abundance of rivals in distant adventure, whereof none was more jealous and more powerful than the Dutch federation which her own good arm had created. Cromwell had read the Dutch a lesson in 1653, and had imposed upon them restrictions which, if observed, would have checked their encroachments on English trade; but the Dutch not only evaded these obligations, but added to this delinquency wanton aggression both on the Guinea Coast and in the East Indies. The African Company at once commenced reprisals on the Gold Coast, and an expedition against the New Netherlands of America captured New Amsterdam and gave it its now famous name of New York.

Meanwhile the complaints of English merchants were willingly heard by both king and Parliament. Charles had received no great kindness in his exile from the oligarchical faction which dominated the Dutch Republic; and now that the same faction had stripped the House of Nassau of its high dignities, to the prejudice of his nephew William, he was not sorry for the opportunity of revenge. Parliament voted liberal supplies for the war. A new regiment, called the Admiral's regiment, was raised by the Duke of York for service on board ship; large drafts were taken from the two regiments of Guards for the same purpose, and on the 3rd of June, James, Duke of York, won with them a great naval action off Lowestoft.

But there were English soldiers outside England who were troubled by this war. The descendants of the volunteers, who had followed Morgan in 1572 and had won an imperishable name under Francis Vere, were still in the Dutch service and were now comprised in seven regiments, three of them English and four Scotch, numbering in all three-and-fifty companies. As soon as war was declared the Pensionary De Witt forced upon the United Provinces a resolution that the British regiments must either take the oath of allegiance to the States-General or be instantly cashiered. This was the reward offered by the Dutch Republic to the brave foreigners who, with their predecessors, had done her better service than she could ever repay. Dismissal from the service meant ruin to the unfortunate officers, and want and misery to the men.

Many Dutchmen were ashamed of the resolution, but they passed it; and it remained only to be seen whether British loyalty would stand the test. The English officers hesitated not a moment. They refused point blank to swear fealty to Holland, and were ruthlessly turned adrift. By the help of the English Ambassador, however, they made their way to England and were presently formed into the Holland regiment, which now ranks as the Third of the Line and is known from the facings which it has worn for more than two centuries, by the honoured name of the Buffs. [1]

The Scottish regiments behaved very differently. Though Charles was a Stuart and a Scot, only two officers had the spirit to follow the English example. The rest, who at first had made great protestation of loyalty, remained with their Dutch masters and, like all shamefaced

1 For the return of the Buffs to England see the *Holland Papers* (Record Office), Bundles 233-235.

converts, professed exaggerated love for the Dutch service and extravagant willingness to invade Great Britain if required. A century hence these regiments will be seen begging in vain to be received into the British service, and only accepted at last, after enduring sad insult from the Dutch, in time to become not the Fourth but the Ninety-Fourth of the Line. The corps finally ceased to exist in 1815, while the Buffs are with us to this day. It was a hard fate, but there is a nemesis even for unfaithful regiments.

In 1666 Louis the Fourteenth, grasped an opportunity for furthering his darling project of extending his frontier to the Rhine, threw in his lot with the Dutch and declared war against England. The time is worthy of remark. For a century England in common with all Europe had abandoned traditional friendships and enmities, and sought out new allies by the guidance of religious sentiment. All this was now at an end, and the old jealousy of France was strong throughout the British Nation. But though the people were in earnest, the king was not; the policy of keeping France in check was after two years abandoned, and Charles II, like a true Stuart, sold himself to Louis the Fourteenth. False, wrong-headed, and unpatriotic, the dynasty was already preparing for itself a second downfall.

The next step was a declaration of war by France and England against Holland. One hundred and fifty thousand men, under the three great captains, Turenne, Condé and Luxemburg, with Louis in person at the head of all, swept down upon the United Provinces, mastered three of them almost without resistance, and actually crossed the Rhine. Six thousand English, grouped around a nucleus from the Guards, served with them under the command of James, Duke of Monmouth, and among the officers was a young captain named John Churchill. He had been born in 1650, less than three months before the Battle of Dunbar during the 3rd English Civil War, had been page to the Duke of York, and had received through him an ensigncy in the King's Guards. He had seen his first service, as became an English officer, in savage warfare at Tangier; he now enjoyed his first experience of a scientific campaign under the first general of the day.

Soon he became known to Turenne himself not only as the handsomest man in the camp, but as an officer of extraordinary gallantry, coolness, and capacity. As Morgan had won the great captain's eulogy at Ypres, so did young Churchill at Maestricht; and it is worthy of note that on both of the two occasions when an English contingent served under Turenne the most brilliant little action of the war was the work of the red-coats.

But on the Dutch side also there was a young man, born in the same year as Churchill, who was to show lesser qualities indeed as an officer, though, as his opportunity permitted him, perhaps hardly inferior qualities as a man. William of Orange, long excluded by the jealousy of faction from the station and the duties of his rank, with firm resolution and unshaken nerve assumed the command of the United Provinces, and began the great work of his life, the work which was to be finally accomplished by the handsome English soldier in the enemy's camp, of taming the insolence of the French.

It is unnecessary to dwell further on the story of this campaign. The courage of William sufficed to tide Holland over the moment of supreme danger; and, the crisis once passed, Austria and Spain, alarmed at the designs of Louis, hastened to her assistance. Charles made peace with the Dutch in 1674, and, while declining to withdraw the English troops in the French service, promised to recruit them no further. Churchill came home to be colonel of the Second Foot; and from the troops disbanded at the close of the war, were formed three English regiments for the service of the Prince of Orange. Among their officers was James Graham of Claverhouse. We shall meet with him again, and we shall see two of the regiments also return in due time, like their prototype, the Buffs, to take their place in the English infantry of the Line.

With the treaty of 1674 the wars of Charles the Second came to an end. It was not that the people of England were unwilling to fight. They were heart and soul against the French; and the Commons cheerfully voted large sums for army and fleet while the war lasted, asking only that the money might be expended on its legitimate object. But the crookedness and untrustworthiness of the king were fatal to all military enterprise, and indeed to all honest administration. Though the military force of England was far too small for the safety of her possessions abroad, Parliament never ceased to denounce the evils of standing armies, and to clamour for the disbanding of all regiments. In the days of Cromwell the burden of the red-coats had been grievous to be borne, but Oliver had at all events made England respected in Europe.

Charles sought to impose a like burden, but without sympathy for England's quarrels, and without care for England's glory. He made shift, nevertheless, to keep his existing regiments throughout his reign, and in 1680 even to add another to them for the service of Tangier. In 1684 that ill-fated possession, having cost many thousands of lives and witnessed as gallant feats of arms as ever were wrought by English soldiers, was finally abandoned; though not before the English had learned one secret of Oriental warfare. In March 1663, after long endurance of incessant harassing attacks from the Moors, the governor, who had hitherto stood on the defensive, took the initiative and launched the Royal Dragoons straight at them.

So signal was the success of this first venture that it was repeated a fortnight later by the same regiment, and renewed on a grander scale after two months by a sally of the whole garrison, which after desperate fighting ended once more in victory. So much at least must be recorded of this first long lost settlement in Africa.[2] The new regiment, which had arrived too late for fighting, came home to take rank as the Fourth of the Line and to remain with us to this day.

In truth the little army, which Parliament so bitterly hated, was busy enough from the day of the king's accession to the day of his death. In regiments or detachments it fought in Tangier, in Flanders, and in the West Indies; it did marines' duty in four great naval actions, one of them the fiercest ever fought by the English, and it suppressed an insurrection in Scotland and a rebellion in Virginia. The reign gave it a foretaste of the work that lay before it in the next two centuries, and showed good promise for the manner in which that work would be done. Charles died on the 6th of February 1685. His brother James, who succeeded him, was a man of stronger military instincts than any English king since Henry the Eighth. He had served through four campaigns under Turenne and through two more with the Spaniards, and his narrative of his wars shows that he had studied the military profession with singular industry and intelligence of observation.

Nor was he less interested in naval affairs. He had commanded an English fleet in two great actions without discredit as an admiral, and with signal honour as a brave man. Moreover, he felt genuine pride in the prowess alike of the English sailor and the English soldier. Finally he had shown uncommon ability and diligence as an administrator.

The Duke of Wellington a century and a half later spoke with the highest admiration of the system which James had established at the Office of Ordnance, and actually restored it, as Marlborough had restored it before him, when he himself became master-general. The Admiralty again acknowledges that his hand is still felt for good in the

---

2. The historian of the Second regiment of Foot has printed a great deal of matter respecting Tangier. Details will also be found in Clifford Walton's *History of the British Standing Army.*.

Scale of half a Mile

0 ¼ ½

Sketch of the
BATTLE of SEDGEMOOR
July 6th 1685.

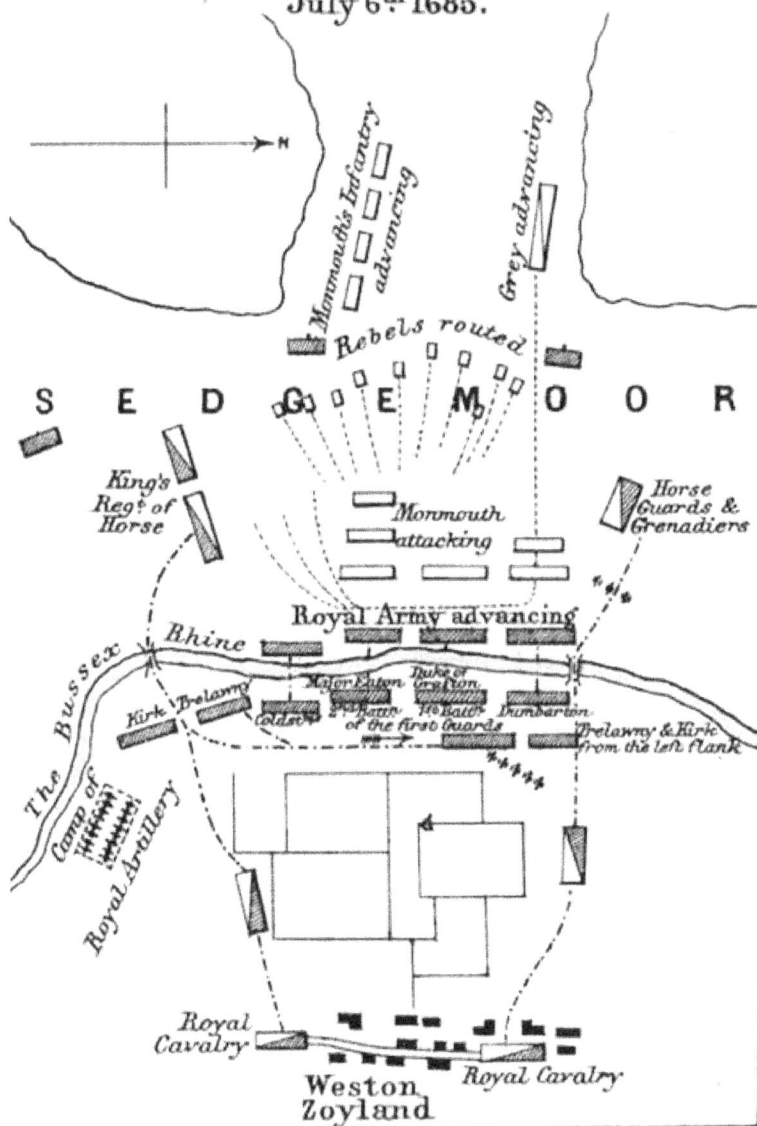

N

Monmouth's Infantry advancing

Grey advancing

Rebels routed

S E D G E M O O R

King's Regt of Horse

Monmouth attacking

Horse Guards & Grenadiers

Royal Army advancing

The Bussex Rhine

Kirk Trelawny

Coldstm

Major Eaton 2d Battn of the first Guards

Duke of Grafton 1st Battn Dumbarton

Trelawny & Kirk from the left flank

Camp of Royal Artillery

Royal Cavalry

Weston Zoyland

Royal Cavalry

direction of the navy. In fact, whatever his failings, James was an able, painstaking, and conscientious public servant, and as such has no little claim to the gratitude of the nation.

So far then the succession of a diligent and competent administrator to the shrewd but incorrigibly idle Charles promised advantages that were obvious enough. But there was another side to the question. Parliament had requited James's services to the public by excluding him as an avowed Catholic from all public employment, whether civil or military; and James was a narrow-minded, a vindictive, and, like all the Stuarts, essentially a wrong-headed man. Though valuable as the head of a department, he was totally unfit to administer a kingdom; though not devoid of constancy and patience in adversity, he was swift and insatiable in revenge; though ambitious of military fame, proud of English valour, and not without jealousy for English honour, he saw no way to the greatness which he coveted in Europe except by the overthrow of English liberty. He longed to interfere effectively abroad, but with England crushed under his heel, not free and united at his back.

So he too sold himself to France, hoping to consolidate his power by her help and to turn it in due time to her own hurt; and meanwhile he sought to strengthen himself by the maintenance of a standing army. For this design Monmouth's insurrection of 1685 afforded sufficient excuse. [3] The opportune return of the garrison of Tangier had already added two regiments of Foot and one of Horse to the English establishment; and James seized the occasion of the outbreak to summon the six British regiments, three of them Scottish and three English, from Holland. These, though they presently returned to William's service, secured for two of their number on the invasion of England in 1688 the precedence of Fifth and Sixth of the Line.

Simultaneously twelve new regiments of infantry and eight of cavalry were raised under the same pretext. Of the foot the first was an Ordnance-regiment, designed like the firelocks of the New Model to act as escort to the artillery, and was called from its armament the Regiment of Fusiliers. It is still with us as the Seventh of the Line. The remainder of the foot, some of them formed round the nucleus of independent garrison-companies, also abide with us, numbered the Eighth to the Fifteenth. [4] Of the cavalry six were regiments of horse,

3. No reader, I am confident, will blame me for leaving him alone with his Macaulay for the account of this insurrection.
4. It is worthy of note that but two of these regiments were raised in the districts indicated by their present titles, viz., the 11th (North Devon) and 12th (East Suffolk).

and are now known as the First to the Sixth Regiments of Dragoon Guards; the remaining two, which are now numbered the Third and Fourth, after having been successively dragoons and light dragoons, have finally become the two senior regiments of hussars. Add to these thirty independent companies of foot, borne for duties in garrison, and it will be seen that King James's army was increasing with formidable speed.

The king himself found genuine delight, not in the sinister spirit of an oppressor but in the laudable pride of a soldier, in reviewing his troops. In August 1685 he inspected ten battalions and twenty squadrons which were in camp at Hounslow, and wrote to his son-in-law, William of Orange, with significant satisfaction of their efficiency. In November he met Parliament, and required of it the continuance of the standing army in lieu of the militia. The courtiers had received their cue, and pointed to the flight of the western militia before Monmouth's raw levies as proof sufficient of its untrustworthiness. The fact indeed was self evident. But Parliament was not disposed to welcome a royal speech which submitted no further measures than the maintenance of a standing army and the admission of popish officers to command therein. The memories of Oliver and of his major-generals was still vivid, and the revocation of the edict of Nantes was but a month old. Red-coats as saints had been bad; red-coats as papists would doubtless be worse.

Edward Seymour, the head of that historic house, put the matter as Englishmen love to put it. The militia, he confessed, was in an unsatisfactory state, but it might be improved, and with this and the navy the country would be secure; but a standing army there must not be. Then as now, it will be observed, the House of Commons never stinted the navy, nor doubted its ability to repel invasion; and then as now it refused to remember that the British possessions are not bounded by the British Isles, and that a successful war is something more than a war of defence. But unfortunately it had but too good ground for opposing the king in this case. The debate lasted long. James had asked for £1,400,000 for the army; the Chancellor of the Exchequer expressed his willingness to accept £1,200,000; the House voted £700,000, and even then declined to appropriate the sum to any specific purpose.

James was greatly annoyed. He answered the note of the Commons with a reprimand, and prorogued Parliament; nor did he summon it again during the remainder of his reign. He then concentrated from thirteen to sixteen thousand men at Hounslow Heath, and kept

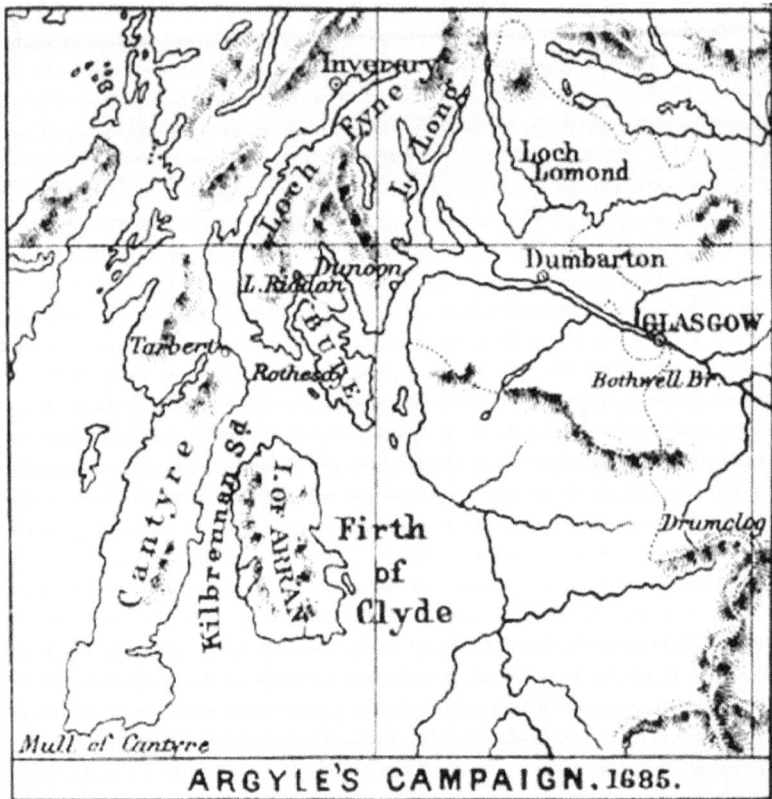

Invergry
Loch Fyne
L. Long
Loch Lomond
Dunoon
L. Ridan
Dumbarton
GLASGOW
Tarbert
Bute
Rothesay
Bothwell Br
Cantyre
Kilbrennan Sd
I. OF ARRAN
Firth of Clyde
Drumclog
Mull of Cantyre

ARGYLE'S CAMPAIGN. 1685.

them encamped there for three years in the hope of overawing London. Never did man make a more complete mistake. The Londoners, after their first alarm had passed away, soon discovered that the camp was a charming place of amusement. A new generation had sprung up since a Parliamentary colonel had held a sham fight to compensate the people for the loss of the sports of May-day, and there was a certain novelty in military display. Hounslow camp became the fashion, and the lines were thronged with a motley crowd of all classes of the people; for then as now the women loved a red-coat, and where the women led the men followed them. The troops were doubtless well worth seeing, for James flattered himself that they were the best paid, the best equipped, and the most sightly in Europe.

Still, merry as the camp might be, there were not wanting signs of a graver spirit beneath the new redcoats. There were early rumours of quarrels between protestant and catholic soldiers, ominous to the catholic officers whom James had set in command against the law. Agitators scattered tracts appealing to the army to stand up in defence of the liberties of England and the protestant religion; and the Londoners perceived, what James did not, that consciences cannot be bought for eight pence a day, nor flesh and blood extinguished by a red coat and facings. The Buffs had been the earliest English volunteers in the cause of liberty and Protestantism; the Royal Scots had rolled back papistry under the Lion of the North, and, as if one Presbyterian regiment were not sufficient, there was another, just brought into England for the first time from Scotland, and known by its present name of the Scotch or Scots Guards.

Again, monks in the habit of their Order were among the visitors to the camp; and it was easy to ask how long it was since such men had been seen in England, and what was the cause of their disappearance. Cromwell's soldiers had made short and cruel work of monks in Ireland; yet soldiers, only one generation younger, were to be called upon to fight against their kith and kin for a king who openly favoured them, a king, too, who in the face of all law openly thrust papists into all places of authority.

It was not long before the seed sown by the agitators began to bear fruit. When the seven bishops who had refused to read the declaration which suspended the penal laws against Catholics were committed to the Tower, (June 1688), the guards drank their health; and when the news of their acquittal reached Hounslow Heath, it was received by the army with boisterous delight. In alarm James broke up the

117

camp and scattered the regiments broadcast over the country. Having thus isolated them he attempted to work upon them separately, and selected as the first subject for this experiment Lord Lichfield's Regiment, known to us as the Twelfth Foot. The men were drawn up on Blackheath in the king's presence, and were informed that they must either sign a pledge to carry out the royal policy of indulgence towards catholic's, or leave his service forthwith.

Whole ranks without hesitation took him at his word, and grounded their arms, while two officers and a few privates, all of them Catholics, alone consented to sign. James stood aghast with astonishment and disgust. Dismissal meant something more than mere exclusion from the army; it carried with it the forfeiture of all arrears of pay and of the price of the officers' commissions, but neither men nor officers took account of that. James eyed them in silence for a time, and then bade them take up their arms. "Another time," he said, " I shall not do you the honour to consult you."

Foiled in England, James turned, as his father had turned before him, to Ireland. The Irish speak of the curse of Cromwell; they might more justly speak of the curse of the Stuarts, for no two men have brought on them such woe as Charles and James. Already, in 1686, the king had sent a degenerate Irishman, the Earl of Tyrconnel, to ensure popish ascendency at any rate in Ireland; and no better man could have been found for such mischievous work than lying Dick Talbot. The army in Ireland consisted at the time of his arrival of about seven thousand men: within a few months Tyrconnel, by wholesale dismissal of all protestants, had turned it upside down.

Five hundred men were discharged from a single regiment on the ground that they were of inferior stature, and their places shamelessly filled by ragged, half-trained Irish, beneath them both in size and quality. In all four thousand soldiers were broken, stripped of the uniforms which they had bought by the stoppage of their pay, and dismissed half-naked to go whither they would. Three hundred protestant officers shared a like fate in circumstances of not less hardship. Many of them had fought bravely for the Stuarts in past days, the majority had purchased their commissions, yet all alike were turned adrift: in ruin and disgrace. The disbanded took refuge in Holland, whence they presently returned under the colours of William of Orange, with such feelings against the Irish as may be guessed.

But James did not stop here. He now conceived the notion of surrounding himself with Irish battalions, and of moulding the English regiments to his will by kneading into them a leaven of Irish recruits. When we reflect that it was just such an importation of Irish that had turned all England against his father, we can only stand amazed at such folly. The English held the Irish for aliens and enemies; they knew them as a people who for centuries had risen in massacre and rebellion whenever the English garrison had been weakened, and that had sunk again into abject submission as soon as England's hands were free to suppress them. They did not know them, in spite of their occasional gallant resistance to Cromwell, as a great fighting race. They had not read, or, reading, had not believed, the testimony of Robert Munro to their merits as soldiers. [5] Lastly and chiefly the Irish were Catholics and the English Protestants.

The resentment against the new policy soon made itself manifest. The Duke of Berwick, the king's natural son, who had been appointed colonel of the Eighth Foot, gave orders that thirty Irish recruits should be enlisted in the regiment. The men said flatly that they would not serve with them, and the lieutenant-colonel with five of his captains openly remonstrated with the duke against the insult. They had raised the regiment, they said, at their own expense for the king's service, and could procure as many English recruits as they wanted; rather than endure to have strangers forced upon them they would beg leave to resign their commissions. James was furious. He tried the six officers by a court-martial, which sentenced them to be cashiered; but the culprits none the less received the sympathy and applause of the whole nation. The prevalent feeling against the Irish found vent in a doggerel ballad, known, from the gibberish of its burden, by the name of *Lillibulero*. Partly from the nature of its contents, still more probably from the rollicking gaiety of its tune, [6] it became a great favourite with the army, and if we may judge from Captain Shandy's partiality for it, was the most popular marching song of the red-coats in Flanders.

But meanwhile William of Orange had received his invitation to come with an armed force for the delivery of England from the Stuarts, and for some months had been making preparations for an invasion. It was long before James awoke to his danger, but when at last he perceived it he hastened to strengthen the army. Commissions were issued for the raising of new regiments, of which two are still with us as the Sixteenth and Seventeenth of the Line, and of new companies

5. *Expedition*, vol. ii.
6. The tune, which is in the key of G major and in 6/4 time, may be found in modern editions of *Tristram Shandy*. It is admirably suited for fifes and drums.

I   II

Bristol Channel

A

BRISTOL
Keynsham
Bath
Pensford
Bradford
Phillips Norton
Melksham
Frome
Westb
Wells   Shepton Mallett   Warmin
Glastonbury
Bridgwater   Bruton   Hindo
Weston   Sedgemoor
Zealand   Somerton
Taunton   Wincanton
     Ilchester   Shaft
R. Exe   Yeovil   Sherborne
Tiverton   Chard   Crewkerne
     Blan
Honiton
Axminster
B   EXETER   Lyme   Bridport   Dorchester
     Wareham
Newton
Abbot
Totness   Tor Bay
Brixham

Scale o

Hale's Fall of the Stewarts.

I   II

March of the Duke of
Prince o

III   IV   SI.

OXFORD

St. Albans

Watford

Wantage

Marlow

Uxbridge

Maidenhead

LONDON

Slough

arlborough   Hungerford   READING   Windsor   Hounslow   A

Newbury   Oakingham   Staines

Chertsey   Kingston

Esher

Basingstoke   Odiham

Whitchurch   GUILDFORD

Andover   Farnham

Amesbury

Stockbridge   Alton

Aylesford

SALISBURY   WINCHESTER   Haslemere

Romsey   Petersfield

Midhurst

Bishops Waltham

Southampton

Ringwood   Fareham

ristchurch   Portsmouth   Chichester   B

ISLE of WIGHT

Map to illustrate
THE CAMPAIGNS OF
1685 and 1688
in the West of England

Miles

50   70   80   90   100

III

...mouth. 1685 --------

...range. 1688 ————

for existing regiments. Four thousand men in all were added to the English establishment; three thousand were summoned from Ireland, and as many more from Scotland; and James reckoned that he could meet the invader with forty thousand men.

On the 2nd of November William, after one failure, got his expedition safely to sea, and by a feint movement induced James to send several regiments northward to meet a disembarkation in Yorkshire. These regiments were hastily recalled on the intelligence that the armament had passed the Straits of Dover steering westward, and fresh orders were given for concentration at Salisbury.

In a short time twenty-four thousand men were assembled at the new rendezvous, but before James could join them, he received news that Lord Cornbury, the heir of his kinsmen the Hydes, had deserted to the enemy. Cornbury had attempted to take his own regiment, the Royal Dragoons, and two regiments of horse with him; but officers and men became suspicious, and with the exception of a few who fell into the hands of William's horse and took service in his army, all returned to Salisbury. Before setting out for the camp James summoned his principal officers to him—Churchill, since 1683 Lord Churchill, and recently promoted lieutenant-general; Henry, Duke of Grafton, colonel of the First Guards; Kirke and Trelawny, colonels of the Tangier Regiments. One and all swore to be faithful to him; and the King left London for Salisbury.

Arrived there, he learned from Lord Feversham, his general-in-chief, that though the men were loyal the officers were not to be trusted. It is said that Feversham proposed to dismiss all that he suspected and promote sergeants in their stead. His suspicions proved to be just. Within a week Churchill, Grafton, Kirke, and Trelawny had all deserted to the Prince of Orange. Other officers were less open in their treachery; and it is said that one battalion of the Foot Guards was led into William's camp by its sergeants and corporals. The desertion of his own children finally broke the spirit of James. On the 11th of December he signed an order for the disbandment of the army, and took to flight; and on the 16th he returned to London to find on the following night that the battalions of the Prince of Orange were marching down St. James's Park upon Whitehall. The old colonel of the Coldstream Guards, Lord Craven, though now in his eightieth year, was for resistance, but James forbade him. The Coldstream Guards filed off, and a Dutch regiment mounted guard at Whitehall. Five days later James left England forever.

CHAPTER 14

Regimental Organisation and Equipment

Before entering on the reign of William we must pause for a time to study the interior administration of the army. The reign of the two last Stuarts is rightly considered as marking the end of a period of English general history—the final fall of the old monarchy first overthrown with King Charles the First. But in regard to military history the case is different. It is a critical time of uncertainty during which the army, a relic barely saved from the ruins of a military government, struggled through twenty-eight years of unconstitutional existence, hardly finding permission at their close to stand on the foundation which Charles and James, using materials left by Cromwell, had made shift to establish for it. Precarious as that foundation was, it received little support for nearly a century, and little more even in the century that followed, thanks to the blind jealousy of the House of Commons. It will therefore be convenient at this point to examine it once for all.

Beginning, therefore, at the top, it must be noted that the first commander-in-chief under the restored monarchy was a subject, George Monk, Duke of Albemarle. His appointment was inevitable, for he had already held that command as the servant of the Parliament over the undisbanded New Model, and he was the only man who could control that army. Charles, in fact, lay at his mercy when he landed in 1660, and could not do less than confirm him in his old office. The powers entrusted to Monk by his commission were very great. He had authority to raise forces, to fix the establishment, to issue commissions to all officers executive and administrative, and to frame Articles of War for the preservation of discipline; he signed all warrants for expenditure of money or stores, and, in a word, he exerted the sovereign's powers as the sovereign's deputy in charge of the army.

On his death in January 1670, Charles, by the advice of his brother James, did not immediately appoint his successor, and though in 1674 he issued a circular to all officers of horse and foot to obey the Duke of Monmouth, yet he expressly reserved to himself many of the powers formerly made over to Monk. Finally, when in 1678 he appointed Monmouth to be captain-general, he withheld from him the title of commander-in-chief. On Monmouth's disgrace in 1679 Charles appointed no successor, but became his own commander-in-chief, an example which was duly followed by James the Second and William the Third. Thus the supreme control of the army, with powers far greater than have been entrusted to any English commander-in-chief of modern times, continued at first practically the same as it had been made by Oliver Cromwell. It was exclusively in military hands.

The special branch of military administration in the hands of the commander-in-chief was that relating to the men. The care of material of war was committed to the ancient and efficient Office of Ordnance. At the Restoration the old post of Master of the Ordnance was revived with the title of master-general; and in 1683 the department was admirably reorganised, as has been seen, by the Duke of York. At the head stood, of course, the master-general; next under him were two officers of two distinct branches, the lieutenant-general and the surveyor-general. The lieutenant-general was charged with the duty of estimating the amount of stores required for the navy and the army, and of making contracts for the supply of the same; he was also responsible for the maintenance of marching trains for service in the field, and for the general efficiency of the artillery both as regards guns and men. His first assistant was named the master-gunner. The surveyor-general was responsible for the custody and care of all stores, and for all services relative to engineering; his first assistant was called the principal engineer.

Transport of ordnance by land was the care of a wagon-master, transport by water of a purveyor. The laboratory was committed to a fire-master, whose duties included the preparation of fireworks for festive occasions. The only weak point of the office was the exclusiveness of its jurisdiction over artillery and engineers, which was carried to such a pitch that all commissions in the two corps were signed by the master-general, though that functionary and his staff received their own commissions from the commander-in-chief.

I turn next to the department of finance. Here in place of the old treasurers at war there was created a new officer called the paymaster-general. Parliament, I must remind the reader, never recognised the existence of the army under the Stuarts, nor voted a sixpence expressly for its service. The force was paid out of the king's privy purse, or, in the case of James, out of sums intended for the payment of the militia. Thus the House of Commons through sheer perversity lost its hold upon the paymaster-general, and when it came to examine his office a whole century later, found, as shall be told in place, a system of corruption and waste which is almost incredible.

The first paymaster-general, Sir Stephen Fox, received a salary of four hundred pounds a year, but this he soon supplemented by becoming practically a farmer of a part of the revenue. Knowing that Charles was chronically deficient in cash, he undertook to advance funds on his own private credit for the weekly pay of the army, in consideration of a commission of one shilling in the pound. At the end of every four months he applied to the Treasury for reimbursement, and if his claims were not immediately satisfied, he received eight *per cent* on the debt owing to him, thus making a very handsome profit. This system was discontinued in 1684, but the deduction, or poundage as it was called, was still levied on the army, for no reason whatever, for a full century and a half. For the care of all other military expenses there was an office called by the old title of Treasurer of the Armies.

So much for the broad divisions of the administration, under the three heads of men, military stores, and finance. It is now necessary to trace the rise of a new department, which was destined to give to civilians the excessive share that they still enjoy in the direction of military affairs. While Charles the Second was yet an exile in Flanders in 1657, he had appointed a civilian, Sir Edward Nicholas, who had been Secretary of Council to Charles the First, to be his Secretary at War. It was not uncommon for such civilian secretaries [1] to be attached to a general's staff, and we have already seen John Rushworth taking the field with the New Model as secretary to the Council of War.

After the Restoration, and within six months of the date of Monk's commission, one Sir William Clarke was appointed to be secretary to the forces. Though a civilian, he received a commission couched in military terms, which were preserved for fully a century unchanged, bidding him obey such orders as he should from time to time receive

---

1. It is possible that there was difficulty in finding ready writers among the military, and still more difficulty in persuading them to unite sword and pen.

from the king, or the general of the forces for the time being, according to the discipline of war. In effect he was a civilian wholly subordinated to the military authorities and subject to military discipline so far as that discipline existed; little more, indeed, than a secretary to the commander-in-chief. His services were not estimated at a very high rate, for he received at first but ten shillings, and after 1669 one pound a day, as salary for himself and clerks. The appointment was of so personal a nature that Clarke accompanied Monk to sea in 1666, and was killed in the naval battle of the 1st of June, the first and last secretary at war who has fallen in action.

Monk then applied for the services of one Matthew Lock, whom he knew to be a good clerk, and Lock was appointed to be Clarke's successor with the title of sergeant or secretary at war. There is not a letter from him to be found in the State Papers until after Monk's death, which is sufficient proof that he was a person of no great importance; but in 1676, when there was no longer a single commander-in-chief, he was entrusted with the removal of quarters, the relief of the established corps, the despatch of convoys, and even with authority to quarter troops in inns, all of which duties had been previously fulfilled by military men. Thus early and insidiously arose once more that civil interference with military affairs which had with such difficulty been thrown off at the establishment of the New Model. The system was wholly unconnected with any question of Parliamentary control, for Parliament would have nothing to do with the standing army. Most probably it was due simply to the indolence of the king, who would neither do the work of commander-in-chief himself nor appoint any other man to do it for him. Thus the army was placed once and for all under the heel of a civilian clerk.

The staff at headquarters was based on the model of that which had prevailed under Cromwell, though of course on a scale reduced to the minute proportions of the army. The duties must, at first, have been within the scope of a very few officials, and it is probable that Monk required little assistance. There was, however, a commissary of the musters, to whom in 1664 a scoutmaster-general, or head of the intelligence department, was added. The business of foreign intelligence in all its branches, diplomatic, naval, and military, had been conducted with admirable efficiency during the Protectorate by the Secretary of State, John Thurloe, but Pepys remarked a sad falling away in this department after the Restoration, due, as he admits, to the scanty allowance of funds allotted to the service. Charles was not the man to face the difficulties of establishing a great administrative office on a sound basis.

James, on the other hand, began to grapple with them very early after his accession. He strengthened the staff by the addition of adjutants and quartermasters-general of horse and foot, and strove hard to improve the efficiency of the office; but his time was too short and his distractions too manifold to permit him to do the work thoroughly. Had he reigned for ten years, his familiarity with the system of Louvois and his own administrative ability might have reduced our military system once for all to order. It is not too much to say that his expulsion was in this respect the greatest misfortune that ever befell the army.

Even he, however, would have found it a hard task to overcome the obstacles raised by Parliament, namely, the difficulties of regular payment of wages and of maintaining discipline. It was impossible to enforce military law on the troops, since Parliament steadily withheld its sanction to the same. [2] Nothing therefore remained but the civil law. A soldier who struck his superior officer or got drunk on guard could legally only be haled before the civil magistrate for common assault or for drunkenness, while if he slept on his post or disobeyed orders or deserted he was subject to no legal penalty whatever. Parliament never seems to ha\e been the least alive to the danger of such a state of things, nor to have weighed it against its fixed resolution not to recognise the standing army.

As a matter of fact, however, military offences seem to have been punished as such throughout the reign of Charles, though without ostentation; and discipline appears to have been maintained without serious difficulty. The number of the troops was, after all, but small; many of the men were already inured to obedience; the traditions of Oliver and of George Monk were still alive; and the men probably accepted service with a tacit understanding that they were subject to different conditions from the civilian. But when the three regiments returned from foreign service and savage warfare at Tangier, and Monmouth's rebellion had brought about a multiplication of regiments, the situation was altogether changed. James, who knew the value of discipline, determined to arrogate the powers that Parliament denied to him, but, like all weak men, endeavoured to effect his purpose by

---

2. But indeed I have failed to discover by what legal authority martial law was enforced on the Parliamentary troops in the Civil War. There seems to have been no effort to give so much as a semblance of legality to the power of the generals.

half measures.

To secure the punishment of certain deserters he packed the Court of King's Bench with unscrupulous men; and though the culprits were hanged, discipline was only preserved at the cost of the integrity of the courts of law, a proceeding which damaged him greatly both in the Army and the country at large. It will presently be seen how this question of discipline was forced upon Parliament in a fashion that allowed of no further trifling.

The subject of pay opens a melancholy chapter in the history of English administration. It has already been related that Charles the Second let out the payment of the army to a contractor for a commission of a shilling in the pound. This commission of course came out of the pockets of officers and men; they paid, in fact, a tax of five per cent for the privilege of receiving their wages, and this not to the State, to which the officers still pay sometimes an equal amount under the name of income-tax, but for the benefit of a private individual.

If the mulcting of the army had ended there, the evil would not have been so serious, but as a matter of fact it was but one drop in a vast ocean of corruption. I have already alluded to the immense service wrought by the Puritans towards integrity of administration, and towards raising the moral standard of the military profession. The destruction of the old traditions and the substitution of new principles was a magnificent stroke, but it was unfortunately premature. The new principles might indeed have endured had they but been cherished and encouraged for another generation, but unfortunately no man better fitted to starve them could have been found than the merry monarch. His difficulties were doubtless very great, but he brought but one principle to meet them, that come what might he must not be bored. His indolent selfishness was masked by an exquisite charm of manner, and being a kind-hearted man, he always heard complaints with a sympathetic word; but to redress them cost more trouble than he could afford.

Any man who would save him trouble was welcome; any shift that would stave off an unpleasant duty was the right one. There was abundance of deserving suitors to be provided for, still greater abundance of importunate favourites to be satisfied; administration was a bore and money was sadly deficient. All difficulties could be solved by the simple process of providing alike the impecunious and the greedy with administrative offices, or, in other words, with licences to plunder the public. If they chose to purchase these offices for money, so much the better for the royal purse. Thus the whole fabric built up during the Commonwealth was shattered almost at a blow.

The effect on the army was immediate. A great many of the returned exiles, including Charles and James themselves, had served in the French Army, where the system of purchasing commissions had never been abandoned, and where the abuses which had been shaken off by the New Model were still in full vigour. The old corrupt traditions had not been killed in thirteen years, and, reviving under the general reaction against Puritan restraint, they sprang quickly into new life. The old military centralisation of Oliver, upheld for a time by Monk, rapidly perished, and what might have still been an army sank into a mere aggregate of regiments, the property of individual colonels, and of troops and companies, the property of individual captains. Every civilian of the military departments hastened to make money at the expense of the officers, and every officer to enrich himself at the cost of the men. The flood-gates so carefully closed by the Puritans were opened, and the abuses of three centuries streamed back into their old channel to flow therein unchecked for two centuries more.

At its first renewal the system of purchase was carried to such lengths that the very privates paid premiums to the enlisting officers; but the practice was speedily checked by Monk in 1663. In March 1684 the system received a kind of royal sanction through the purchase by the king himself of a commission from one officer for presentation to another. Then nine months later Charles suddenly declared that he would permit no further purchase and sale of military appointments. Whether he would have abolished it if he had lived may be doubted, but it is certain that the system continued in full operation under James the Second, gathering strength of course with each new year of existence.

Let me now attempt briefly to sketch the organised system of robbery that prevailed in the military service under the two last of the Stuarts. The study may be unpleasant, but it is less pathological than historic. First, then, let us treat of the officer. On purchasing his commission he paid forthwith one fee to the Secretary at War, and a second, apparently, to one of the Secretaries of State. After the institution of Chelsea Hospital, as to which a word shall presently be said, he paid further five *per cent* on his purchase money towards its funds, the seller of the commission contributing a like proportion from the same sum to the same object. He then became entitled to the pay of his rank, but this by no means implied that it was regularly paid to him.

In the first place, his pay was divided into two parts, termed respectively his subsistence and his arrears, or clearings. The former sum was a proportion of the full pay, which varied according to the grade of the officer, it being obvious that an ensign, for instance, could not subsist if any large fraction was deducted from his daily pittance, whereas a major could be more heavily mulcted and yet not starve. This subsistence was therefore paid, or supposed to be issued, in advance from the pay-office and to be subject to no stoppage. The balance of the full pay, or arrears, was paid yearly after it became due, and after considerable deductions had been made from it. First of these deductions came the poundage, or payment of one shilling in the pound, to the paymaster-general, and the discharge of one day's full pay to Chelsea Hospital. These stoppages were more or less legitimate. Then the commissary-general of the musters stepped in to claim from the officer, as from everyone else in the army, one day's pay, a tax which caused much discontent, and was in 1680 reduced to one-third of a day's pay. Then came a vast number of irregular exactions.

Every commissary of the musters claimed a fee, amounting sometimes to as much as two guineas for every troop or company passed at each muster, which, as musters were taken six times a year, was sufficiently exorbitant. Next the auditors demanded thirty shillings, or eight times their legal fee, for each troop and company on passing the accounts of the paymaster-general. Finally, fees to the exchequer, fees to the treasury, fees for the issue of pay-warrants, fees, in a word, to every greedy clerk who could make himself disagreeable, brought the tale of extortion to an end. Let the reader remember that this system of subsistence and arrears, with the same legitimate deductions and almost equal opportunities for irregular pilfering, was still in force when we began the war of the French Revolution, and let him not wonder that officers of the army will still cherish unfriendly feelings towards the clerks at the War Office. [3]

Now comes the more distressing examinations of the officers' methods of indemnifying themselves. For this purpose let us study the pay of a private sentinel, as he was called, of the infantry of the Line. This consisted, as it had been in Queen Mary's time, and was still to be in King George the Third's, of eight pence a day, or £12: 13:4 a year.

---

3. It should not be forgotten meanwhile, in justice to the clerks, that their salaries were very irregularly paid and that they depended chiefly on their perquisites. We do not realise, in fact, how recently salaries have supplanted fees in the payment of officials.

Of this, sixpence a day, or £9:2:6 a year, was set apart for his subsistence, and was nominally inviolable. The balance, £3:0:10 a year, was called the "gross off-reckonings," which were subject of course to a deduction of five *per cent*, or 12s. 2d., for the paymaster-general, and of one day's pay to Chelsea Hospital, whereby the gross off-reckonings were reduced to £2: 8s. This last amount, dignified by the title of "net off-reckonings," was made over to the colonel for the clothing of the regiment, an item which included not only the actual garments, but also the sword and belt, and as time went on the bayonet and cartridge box. The system, as will be remembered, dated from the days of Queen Elizabeth, when half a crown a week was allowed to the men for subsistence and a total of £4:2:6 deducted for two suits a year.

It is sufficiently plain that the sum now allowed for clothing was insufficient, and that a colonel who did his duty by his men must inevitably be a loser. Moreover, this was not his only expense. The clerical work entailed by his duties demanded assistance, for which he was indeed authorised to keep a clerk, but supplied with no allowance wherewith to pay him. This clerk presently became known as the colonel's agent, and though a civilian and the colonel's private servant, virtually performed the duties of a regimental paymaster.

The results of such an arrangement may easily be guessed. It was not in consonance with military tradition, certainly not in accordance with human nature, that colonels should lose money by their commands, and it is only too certain that they did not. The contractor was called in, and the door was opened wide to robbery at the expense of the soldier. Colonels took commissions or even open bribes from the contractors; the agent took his fee likewise; and in at least one recorded case a colonel actually accepted a bribe from his own agent to give him the contract. It may easily be imagined how the soldiers fared for clothing. But the mischief did not end here. The subsistence-money, though in theory subject to no deduction, was practically at the mercy of the colonel and his agent, who, under various pretexts, appropriated a greater or smaller share of the poor soldier's sixpence. As an additional source of profit, it was not uncommon for colonels to abstain from reporting the vacancy caused by an officer's death, to continue to draw the dead man's pay and to put it into his own pocket.

Captains of companies, with such an example before them, were not slow to imitate it; and from them too the unfortunate soldiers suffered not a little. But their easiest road to plunder was the old beaten track of false musters, which was rendered all the easier by the corruption of the commissaries. Any vacancy in the ranks after one muster was left unfilled until the day before the next muster, and the captain drew pay for an imaginary man during the interval. Or again, the *passe-volant*, old as the days of Hawkwood, made his reappearance at musters and was passed, with or without the collusion of the commissaries, as a genuine soldier. Finally, Charles himself gave countenance after a manner to this fraud by reviving the practice of allowing officers so many imaginary men or permanent vacancies in each troop or company in order to increase their emoluments.

And so the *passe-volant* became naturalised first as a "faggot," and later as a "warrant man" in the infantry and a "hautbois" in the cavalry, and survived to a period well within the memory of living men. [4] The remoter a regiment's quarters from home the grosser were the abuses that prevailed in it, and in Ireland they seem to have passed all bounds. Captains calmly appropriated the entire pay of their companies, and turned the men loose to live by the plunder of the inhabitants. It was a reversion to the evils rampant in Queen Elizabeth's army in the Netherlands, and, in justice to the officers, it must be added that those evils were brought about in both cases by the same cause. Officers were simply forced into dishonesty by the withholding of their own pay by civilian officials in London.

It must not be thought that these scandals passed unnoticed at headquarters. As early as 1663 orders were issued to put a stop to fraudulent musters, and two years later the salaries of the officers of the Ordnance were increased almost threefold to check the sale of places and to diminish the temptation to accept bribes. Similar orders were respectively promulgated from time to time, but with little or no effect; possibly they were issued mainly as a matter of form, to stop the mouth of criticism. The root of the evil is to be traced to the civilian paymaster-general, who from the peculiarity of his position was accountable to no one, and enjoyed total irresponsibility for full forty years.

The king no doubt flattered himself that the men were regularly paid; the abuses took some time to attain to their height, and in the short reign of James the Second it is probable that his attention to military business did somewhat to improve matters. But while Charles was on the throne the paymaster-general did as he pleased. Though wages were nominally paid after each muster, they were often with-

4. The warrant men and hautbois can generally be found in old muster-rolls under the names of John Doe, Richard Roe, and Peter Squib.

held for months, and even for years. Finally, when payment was at last made, it was discharged not in cash but in tallies or debentures which could only be sold at a discount; while the colonels' agents seized the opportunity to deduct a percentage in consideration of the trouble to which they had been subjected to obtain any payment whatever.

So the old foundations of fraud were renovated, and on them was built during the next century and a half a gigantic superstructure of rascality and corruption which is not yet wholly demolished. Let it not be thought that in the seventeenth century such malpractices were either new or confined to England. They were, as I have often repeated, as old almost as the art of war, and they were rampant all over Europe. The excuse of English officers for their dishonesty was always, "It is so in France," and in France, as the history of the French Revolution shows, the old evils endured and throve for another full century.

But the sin and shame of England is, that though she had once put away the accursed thing from her, she returned to it again as the sow to her wallowing in the mire. In 1659 English soldiers were proud of their name and calling; in 1666 it had already become a scandal to be a Life Guardsman. Recruits had been found without difficulty under the Commonwealth to make the military profession, as was the rule in those days, the business of their whole life; but after a very few years of the Stuarts the king was compelled to resort to the pressgang. The status of the soldier was lowered, and has never recovered itself to this day.

I turn from this melancholy tale of retrogression to contemplate the changes made in other departments of the service. Herein it will be most convenient to begin with the regimental organisation and equipment. First, then, let us glance at the cavalry, which at the Restoration appears definitely to have taken precedence as the senior service. The reader will remember that in the New Model the fixed strength of a regiment was six troops of one hundred men, which was reduced in time of peace to an establishment of sixty men. Setting aside the Life Guards, which were independent troops of two hundred gentlemen apiece, the regiment which first occupies our attention is the Blues, which began life with eight troops, each of sixty men. So far there was practically no change, but in 1680 the strength of the Blues was diminished to fifty men in a troop; and in 1687 the newly raised regiments were established at an initial strength of six or seven troops of forty men only.

Finally, as shall presently be seen in the campaigns that lie before us in Flanders, the establishment of a troop for war sinks to fifty men, and the establishment for peace to thirty-six. Here, therefore, is Cromwell's excellent system overthrown. The troop of cavalry is so far weakened as to be not worth assorting into three divisions, one to each of the three officers, and the seeds of enforced idleness are sown, to bear fruit an hundredfold. Hardly less significant is the appointment, in 1661, of regimental adjutants to help the majors in the duties which they had hitherto discharged without assistance.

The equipment of the Horse was likewise altered. The trooper retained the iron head-piece [5] and *cuirass*, the pistols and the sword of the New Model, but he was now further supplied with a carbine, which was slung at his back, and with a cartridge box for his ammunition. The new equipment was served out to the household troops in 1663, and to other regiments of Horse in 1677. It marks a new birth of the futile practice of firing from the saddle, which has wasted untold ammunition with infinitesimal results. As regards horses it was still the rule, which had been little modified during the Civil War, that the trooper should bring with him his own horse; if he had none the king supplied him with one, at an average price, and the money was stopped, if necessary, from the trooper's pay.

The drill still bore marks of Cromwell's influence, for the men were drawn up in three ranks only; and though the attack was opened by the discharge of carbines and pistols, yet it was distinctly laid down that when the fire-arms were empty, there must be no thought of reloading, but immediate resort to the sword. Moreover, although the front was still increased or diminished by the doubling of ranks or files, there were already signs of the manoeuvre by small divisions that was to displace it.

Passing next to the dragoons, the reader will have noticed that this arm was not represented in the original army formed by Charles the Second. Notwithstanding the high reputation which dragoons had enjoyed during the Civil War, it was not until 1672 that a regiment of them was raised, and then only to be disbanded after a brief existence of two years. The Tangier Horse, now called the First Royal Dragoons, was converted into a regiment of dragoons on its return from foreign service in 1684; and four years later there was added to the establishment a Scotch regiment which bears a famous name. It was made up

---

5. Which, however, was soon discarded for the hat, with or without an iron skull-piece beneath it.

in 1681 of three independent troops that had been raised three years before, and was completed by three additional troops, under the name of the Royal Regiment of Dragoons of Scotland. It now ranks as the Second regiment of the Cavalry of the Line, and is known to all the world as the Scots Greys.

Dragoons still preserved their original character of mounted infantry. Twelve men of each troop besides the non-commissioned officers were armed with the halberd and a pair of pistols, while the remainder were equipped with matchlock muskets, bandoliers, and, after 1672, with bayonets. In 1687 this equipment was improved by the substitution of flintlocks for matchlocks, of cartridge boxes for bandoliers, and of buckets, in addition to the old slings, for the carriage of muskets. The tactical unit of the dragoons was still called the company, though at the close of the Civil War often denominated the troop; but the tendency of dragoons to assimilate themselves to horse is seen in the substitution of cornet for ensign as the title of the junior subaltern. This tendency was perhaps the stranger, since the companies of dragoons, eighty men strong, must have presented a favourable contrast to the weak and attenuated troops of horse.

A new description of mounted soldier appeared in 1683, [6] in the shape of the Horse-grenadier. I shall have more to say presently of grenadiers, when treating of the infantry, so it is sufficient to state here that Horse-grenadiers were practically only mounted men of that particular arm, who as a rule linked their horses for action and fought on foot like the dragoons. There were in all three troops of Horse-grenadiers, which were attached to the three troops of Life Guards. Their peculiarity was that the two junior officers of each troop were both lieutenants, instead of lieutenant and cornet.

The infantry, like the cavalry, suffered an alteration in the regimental establishments after the Restoration. The old strength of one hundred and twenty to a company was reduced to one hundred, and in time of peace sank to eighty, sixty, and even fifty men. The number of companies to a battalion was also altered. The First Guards began life with twelve companies; and though for a time the Coldstreamers and newly raised regiments retained the original number of ten, yet twelve gradually became the usual, and after the accession of James the Second, the accepted, strength of a battalion. It must be noted that after 1672 a battalion and a regiment of foot cease to be synonymous

---

6. Some say in 1678, but no sign of them appears in the Army Lists or Commission Registers till 1683.

terms, the First Guards being in that year increased to twenty-four companies and two battalions, a precedent which was soon extended to sundry other regiments.

On the accession of James there was added to the twelve companies of every regiment an additional company of grenadiers. These were established first in 1678, and took their name from the grenade,[7] the new weapon with which they were armed. The hand grenade was simply a small shell of from one to two inches in diameter, kindled by a fuse and thrown by the hand. Hence it was entrusted to the tallest and finest men in the regiment, who might reasonably be expected to throw it farthest.

The white plume, supposed to be symbolic of the white smoke of the fuse, was not apparently used at first as the distinctive mark of grenadiers. They, and the fusiliers likewise, wore caps instead of broad-brimmed hats, to enable them to sling their firelocks over both, shoulders with ease. These caps, which were at first of fur, were soon made of cloth, and assumed the shape of the mitre which Hogarth has handed down to us. Another peculiarity of grenadiers was that they were always armed with firelocks and with hatchets,[8] and that both of their subaltern officers were lieutenants.

Another new branch of the infantry was the regiment of Fusiliers, so called from the fusil or flintlock, as opposed to the matchlock, with which they were armed. They were, in fact, simply an expansion of the companies of firelocks which formed part of the New Model in the department of the Train; they were borne for duty with the artillery specially, and therefore included one company of miners. Miner-companies were armed with long carbines and hammer-hatchets peculiar to themselves, and they had but one subaltern officer, a lieutenant. Like the grenadiers, the fusiliers did not recognise the rank of ensign, and their junior subalterns were therefore called second lieutenants.[9]

It is somewhat remarkable that so much should have been made of a weapon so familiar as the firelock. Men who, like Gustavus Adolphus, saw that the whole future of warfare turned on the fire of musketry, had long accepted its superiority to the matchlock; and George

---

7. Spanish *granada*, a pomegranate. Grenadiers were established in France in 1667.
8. The hatchet was issued for the hewing down of the palisades at the attack of a fortified place. This is one reason why the grenadiers were nearly always told off for the assault of a fortress.
9. But this rank was not confined to them. The Royal Scots at this period possessed second lieutenants in addition to ensigns.

Monk, on marching into London in 1660, had at once ordered the Coldstreamers to return their matchlocks into store and to draw firelocks in their stead. Nor was this preference confined solely to military reformers, for we find the Assemblies of Barbados and Jamaica, remote islands in which old fashions might have been expected to die their hardest, uncompromisingly rejecting the matchlocks prescribed for them by the English Government and insisting on arming themselves with "fusees."

At home, however, jobbery and corruption were doubtless at work, for the Coldstream Guards reverted to the matchlock in 1665. Finally, after many compromises, the Guards were in 1683 armed exclusively with firelocks, while the other regiments carried a fixed proportion, probably not less than one-half, of the superior weapon among their matchlocks.

Correspondingly we find throughout these reigns a steady diminution in the use of the pike. In companies of grenadiers and regiments of fusiliers they were utterly abolished; in other corps the proportion, which had once been one-half, had already sunk at the Restoration to one-third, whence it speedily declined to one-fourth and one-fifth.[10] We find them, however, still in use during the wars of William the Third, and we shall see that they did not want advocates even at the close of the Seven Years' War, to say nothing of the part that they played in the French Revolution. [11] As a weapon for officers it survived for many generations under the form of the half-pike or spontoon, [12] even as the halberd prolonged its life as the peculiar weapon of sergeants. To the officers also was assigned by a singular coincidence the preservation of the memory of the armour which had once been worn by all pikemen; and the gorget survived as a badge of rank on their breasts long after corslet and tassets had vanished from the world.[13]

None the less the pike had received its death-blow through the invention of the bayonet. This new and revolutionary weapon had

10. The allowance in 1692 is fourteen per company.

11. For the reluctance of the French to part with pikes see Belhomme, *L'Armée Française en 1690*. The word *piquet* descends from the time when the pikemen were but a small body in the centre of the battalion, *ibid.*

12. Thus General Cadogan, when virtually commander-in-chief, carried a half-pike at a review of the Guards in June 1722. *Flying Post*, 14th June 1722 (Marlborough died 16th June 1722).

13. The pikemen of the *Guardes Suisses* in France, however, clung to the defensive armour for years after it had been discarded by others, a curious survival of the old glory of the Swiss.

been invented in 1640, when it consisted of a double-edged blade, like a pike-head, mounted on two or three inches of wooden haft, which could be thrust into the barrel of the musket. In this form the bayonet was issued first to the Tangier regiment [14] alone in 1663, and to all the infantry and dragoons in 1673, but only to be withdrawn, until in 1686 it was finally reissued to the Foot Guards. It was not until after the Revolution that bayonets were served out to the whole of the infantry.

In the matter of drill there was little or no change. The front was still increased or diminished by the doubling of ranks and of files, and the file still consisted of six men. The reduction of the numbers of pikemen, however, greatly increased the homogeneity of the infantry and contributed not a little to simplify its movements. Moreover, although the file might consist of six men, it is not likely, considering how far the musket and bayonet had superseded the pike, that the formation for action was greater than three ranks in depth. The platoon is not mentioned in the drill books, the probable reason being that it was not favoured by the French School, in which Charles and James had both of them received their training. But for this, there is every reason to suppose that the army encamped on Hounslow Heath would not have been found behind the times in the matter of exercise and equipment if it could have been transported without change to the field of Blenheim.

Of the artillery there is still little to be said. Until 1682 gunners seem to have enjoyed their original distribution into small, independent bodies, in charge of the various scattered garrisons. Even such small organisation as appeared in the New Model seems to have been lost, and field-guns appear to have been told off to battalions of infantry, or to have been worked by such of the escort of fusiliers as had been trained by the few expert gunners. The artilleryman had long looked upon himself as a superior mortal, [15] but in 1682 he was brought under the Ordnance, subjected to military discipline, and regularly exercised at his duty. The time was not far distant when the organisation of the gunners was to be improved. Of engineers I can

---

14. 2nd Queen's.
15. No better instance of this can be found than in Georg von Frundsberg, the famous *landsknecht*-leader, who once, being in supreme command of an army, took the linstock from a gunner and aimed and fired a gun himself. The "officer commanding artillery" at once came up, cashiered the gunner, and bade Georg look after his men and not meddle with other people's guns.

say no more than the few details already given when describing the Ordnance Office and the fusiliers.

A word remains to be said of the foundation of Chelsea Hospital. It has been told that Queen Mary was the first of our sovereigns who showed any care for old soldiers, and that Elizabeth was intolerably impatient of such miserable creatures. Two generations, however, had bred a softer heart in English sovereigns, and when Charles the Second had been twenty years on the throne, and England was again thronged with maimed and infirm soldiers who had served their time in Tangier, in the West Indies, or in the Low Countries, it was felt to be a reproach that faithful fighting-men should be left to starve or to beg their bread. Kilmainham Hospital in Dublin was the first-fruit of this sentiment, and was founded in 1680; Chelsea followed it in the succeeding year. Sir Stephen Fox, the paymaster-general, was the man who was foremost in the work, and it is to his credit that, having made so much money out of the private soldier, he should have chosen this method of repaying him.

The scheme of the hospital was submitted to the king, who was asked to grant a piece of land for a building. Charles, always gracious, readily complied, and offered the site of St. James's College, Chelsea. "But odso!" he added, "I now recollect that I have already given that land to Mistress Nell here." Whereupon, so runs the story, whether true or untrue, Nell gracefully forewent her grant for so good a purpose; and Chelsea Hospital is the British soldier's to this day.

It is painful to have to add that the officials of the pay-office seem to have begun at once to steal part of the money contributed by the army to its maintenance, though the fact will astonish no reader who has followed me through this chapter. But the friends of the Army have always been few, and the best of them in former times, strange conjunction, were a queen and a harlot. Had they endowed a fund for supplying African negroes with Bibles, or even with mass-books, much would be forgiven them in England; but they thought more of saving old soldiers from want, so Mary Tudor is still Bloody Mary, and Eleanor Gwyn the unspeakable Nell.

LEONAUR

ALSO FROM LEONAUR
AVAILABLE IN SOFTCOVER OR HARDCOVER WITH DUST JACKET

THE FALL OF THE MOGHUL EMPIRE OF HINDUSTAN *by H. G. Keene*—By the beginning of the nineteenth century, as British and Indian armies under Lake and Wellesley dominated the scene, a little over half a century of conflict brought the Moghul Empire to its knees.

LADY SALE'S AFGHANISTAN *by Florentia Sale*—An Indomitable Victorian Lady's Account of the Retreat from Kabul During the First Afghan War.

THE CAMPAIGN OF MAGENTA AND SOLFERINO 1859 *by Harold Carmichael Wylly*—The Decisive Conflict for the Unification of Italy.

FRENCH'S CAVALRY CAMPAIGN *by J. G. Maydon*—A Special Correspondent's View of British Army Mounted Troops During the Boer War.

CAVALRY AT WATERLOO *by Sir Evelyn Wood*—British Mounted Troops During the Campaign of 1815.

THE SUBALTERN *by George Robert Gleig*—The Experiences of an Officer of the 85th Light Infantry During the Peninsular War.

NAPOLEON AT BAY, 1814 *by F. Loraine Petre*—The Campaigns to the Fall of the First Empire.

NAPOLEON AND THE CAMPAIGN OF 1806 *by Colonel Vachée*—The Napoleonic Method of Organisation and Command to the Battles of Jena & Auerstädt.

THE COMPLETE ADVENTURES IN THE CONNAUGHT RANGERS *by William Grattan*—The 88th Regiment during the Napoleonic Wars by a Serving Officer.

BUGLER AND OFFICER OF THE RIFLES *by William Green & Harry Smith*—With the 95th (Rifles) during the Peninsular & Waterloo Campaigns of the Napoleonic Wars.

NAPOLEONIC WAR STORIES *by Sir Arthur Quiller-Couch*—Tales of soldiers, spies, battles & sieges from the Peninsular & Waterloo campaingns.

CAPTAIN OF THE 95TH (RIFLES) *by Jonathan Leach*—An officer of Wellington's sharpshooters during the Peninsular, South of France and Waterloo campaigns of the Napoleonic wars.

RIFLEMAN COSTELLO *by Edward Costello*—The adventures of a soldier of the 95th (Rifles) in the Peninsular & Waterloo Campaigns of the Napoleonic wars.

LEONAUR

ALSO FROM LEONAUR
AVAILABLE IN SOFTCOVER OR HARDCOVER WITH DUST JACKET

AT THEM WITH THE BAYONET *by Donald F. Featherstone*—The first Anglo-Sikh War 1845-1846.

STEPHEN CRANE'S BATTLES *by Stephen Crane*—Nine Decisive Battles Recounted by the Author of 'The Red Badge of Courage'.

THE GURKHA WAR *by H. T. Prinsep*—The Anglo-Nepalese Conflict in North East India 1814-1816.

FIRE & BLOOD *by G. R. Gleig*—The burning of Washington & the battle of New Orleans, 1814, through the eyes of a young British soldier.

SOUND ADVANCE! *by Joseph Anderson*—Experiences of an officer of HM 50th regiment in Australia, Burma & the Gwalior war.

THE CAMPAIGN OF THE INDUS *by Thomas Holdsworth*—Experiences of a British Officer of the 2nd (Queen's Royal) Regiment in the Campaign to Place Shah Shuja on the Throne of Afghanistan 1838 - 1840.

WITH THE MADRAS EUROPEAN REGIMENT IN BURMA *by John Butler*—The Experiences of an Officer of the Honourable East India Company's Army During the First Anglo-Burmese War 1824 - 1826.

IN ZULULAND WITH THE BRITISH ARMY *by Charles L. Norris-Newman*—The Anglo-Zulu war of 1879 through the first-hand experiences of a special correspondent.

BESIEGED IN LUCKNOW *by Martin Richard Gubbins*—The first Anglo-Sikh War 1845-1846.

A TIGER ON HORSEBACK *by L. March Phillips*—The Experiences of a Trooper & Officer of Rimington's Guides - The Tigers - during the Anglo-Boer war 1899 - 1902.

SEPOYS, SIEGE & STORM *by Charles John Griffiths*—The Experiences of a young officer of H.M.'s 61st Regiment at Ferozepore, Delhi ridge and at the fall of Delhi during the Indian mutiny 1857.

CAMPAIGNING IN ZULULAND *by W. E. Montague*—Experiences on campaign during the Zulu war of 1879 with the 94th Regiment.

THE STORY OF THE GUIDES *by G.J. Younghusband*—The Exploits of the Soldiers of the famous Indian Army Regiment from the northwest frontier 1847 - 1900.

www.ingramcontent.com/pod-product-compliance
Lightning Source LLC
Chambersburg PA
CBHW021008090426
42738CB00007B/711